Our Faith Story
Its Telling and Its Sharing

Our Faith Story
Its Telling and Its Sharing

AN EDUCATION IN FAITH

A. Patrick Purnell SJ

National Adviser for Religious Education,
England and Wales

Collins

© 1985 Department of Catholic Education and Formation,
Bishops Conference of England and Wales

ISBN 1 899481 09 5
First Published 1985
Fourth Printing 1991
HarperCollinsPublishers
77-85 Fulham Palace Road
London W6 8JB

Fifth Printing 1995
by Rejoice Publications
19 Wellington Close
Chelmsford
Essex CM1 2EE

Cum permissu superiorum
Nihil obstat **Anton Cowan, censor**
Imprimatur ✠ Rt Rev David Konstant VG
Bishop in Central London
Westminster 15 March, 1985

Cover Design by Jeff Carter
Typographical design by Colin Reed
Original Typesetting by John Swain and Son (Glasgow) Limited
Fifth Printing by J.B Offset

Contents

Contents

Part Two   Sharing our Faith Story

Part Three   Settings

Contents

To Douglas Water

A journey within a journey

Acknowledgements

If I were to acknowledge the names of all the people to whom I am indebted the book would appear simply as an appendix to that list. To all of them I say thank you. In particular, however, I wish to thank

All the members of the National Board of Religious Education Inspectors and Advisers for their encouragement and support

Rt Rev D. Konstant, for his support and encouragement

Monsignor Kevin Nichols, my predecessor, for his wisdom and his writings

Fr Robert Butterworth SJ, for his theological advice

Sr Eileen Carroll, for her work at the initial stages of the project

Miss Nora Hanlon for her experience and guidance, and all the work she has put into the project

Fr Harry Stratton for his support and encouragement and his involvement in the project

Miss Teresa Sallnow for her work on the project; and her critical evaluation of the first draft

Fr James Gallagher, SDB, for his encouragement and critical evaluation of the first draft

Sr Madeleine Cecile Prendergast, similarly, for her encouragement and critical evaluation of the first draft

Mrs Sue Chapman for her continued interest, encouragement and involvement in the project

Mrs Patricia Mackey for producing the first draft

Sr Bernadette O'Donoghue for her constant and patient support in typing and retyping the text

Preface

This is one of the most 'real' books about how people grow in faith that I have ever read. Father Purnell describes his own journey in faith and in so doing provides a basis from which the pattern of the growth in faith of others is explored. Such an unashamedly personal approach gives the book an attractiveness rarely found in educational literature, and an authority quite its own.

I hope the book is widely read by parents, priests, teachers and catechists. It may encourage them to think about their own faith and how they have come to it: it may help them understand where their children, parishioners or pupils are, and how to lead them further along the road of faith; it may give rise to fruitful questioning and, it is hoped, to a deeper life of faith. It exemplifies well the familiar description of catechesis as that process by which an individual is enabled, in the light of God's word, to explore his life's experience, to reflect on it, and so to deepen it.

As indicated in the Foreword, this book is but a stage in a considerable process. As its implications are worked out I hope that further publications and productions will follow, for example, guidelines for a deeper understanding of its major themes, possibly a video for use in parishes, and perhaps a handbook for catechists and leaders.

I am delighted to be able to welcome this book. It is at times moving and inspiring, at times instructive and at times questioning. I believe it may prove both supportive and encouraging to many people, especially parents, priests and professional educators, who are concerned about the growth in faith of those for whom they care.

✠ David Konstant
Department of Christian Doctrine and Formation

Foreword

This is a book about education in faith. It is intended to help us to re-flect on our own faith and how we share it with others. It is the product of a long process of sharing with members of diocesan religious educa-tion teams throughout England and Wales who together comprise the National Board of Religious Education Inspectors and Advisers. In addressing the question how do we help others grow in faith? it opens up new perspectives.

How we first came to realise the presence of God in our lives and what experiences have shaped our faith is for each of us a personal story of discovery through the people and events of our lives. How we might help others discern meaning and grow in faith will be influ-enced by our own faith story and our own living recognition of God active in our own world and experience. Hence the title of this book: *Our Faith Story: Its Telling and Its Sharing.* In it, Father Purnell tells us something of his own faith story. By reflecting on some of the experi-ences which have influenced his own growth in faith from early child-hood to his present position as National Adviser for Religious Educa-tion to the Bishops' Conference of England and Wales, he invites us to see how God has been at work in our lives too. He draws us into a pro-cess of sharing and growing, in the clear conviction that helping adults develop their faith is an essential part of helping children grow in faith. After many years of involvement in religious education Father Purnell is familiar with the strengths of the Catholic school and its limitations. He underlines that growth in faith depends on the inter-play of the activities which go on in home, school and parish, and is concerned that the contribution of the family and of the parish should be affirmed and developed.

The members of the National Board are conscious that they are themselves continually involved in deepening their own faith and developing ways of sharing it. They acknowledge that debate and sometimes disagreement, from which this book has not escaped, are a healthy and necessary part of that process. Nonetheless, within that framework the Board sees that this book is a major contribution to the way we share our faith with others; and it feels confident in using it for that purpose. The process which it illustrates invites groups and individuals to share in it. This may lead them to want to become more involved in helping in the work of deepening faith in everyday life. The Board welcomes all such initiatives and hopes that these people will come forward and join in this work. It therefore welcomes this book and congratulates Father Purnell for writing it.

William Byrne

Chairman
National Board of Religious Education Inspectors and Advisers

March 1985

Introduction

1. Origins

In settling down to write this book I began by thinking of writing a document, an official document about the state of religious education within the Catholic community and its relationship to the rest of the country. However, as I began to reflect on my own abilities and what such a document would have to contain if it was to carry any authority, I realised that such a task was not for me. Nevertheless, I realised that I had been in this line of business a long time and that I had done a lot of speaking and that much of what I was saying I was receiving from my continuous contact with people struggling to help people grow in faith. The concept of an official document receded and I began to consider how best I could respond to the variety of experiences which I had acquired from countless sources; how best I could put down on paper what I was attempting to do when I myself tried to share my faith. What do I, indeed, believe is central to the process of faith-sharing?

I believe that God is present in the whole of creation; deep down in every human being God is there not simply keeping each one in existence but lovingly at work helping each reach that fullness of being which is God's destiny for her/him. When, therefore, I venture to share my faith with another I have to realise that God is already present in the other in ways, perhaps, which may be foreign to my own understanding of God. I came then to realise that faith-sharing required first of all discernment; a sensitivity to the divine. My task was not to give God to anybody but to help people discover God within themselves as the life-giving and love-giving source of their existence. I realised that this must be the key to whatever I wrote. I realised, also, that my understanding of this truth was something which was in the process of growing; sometimes I felt I could understand what it was all about, and at other times I felt that it had slipped away from my grasp. My faith was evolving; I was a pilgrim on the journey of faith. There was no way I could write except within this context.

And so this is the way this book came to be written. It is about sharing faith; it is about searching and asking; about knocking and waiting for the door to be opened.

In the foreword the chairperson of the National Board of Religious Education Inspectors and Advisers has indicated the nature of this book. My predecessor, Mgr Kevin Nichols, was commissioned by the Conference of the Bishops of England and Wales to write a book on the basic theory of religious education. *Cornerstone,* published in 1978, was the fruit of his study and it has become a very important book for all who are involved in the work of religious education, not only in this country but also abroad. In 1981 Bishop Konstant headed a study group which produced *Signposts and Homecomings* which was subtitled 'The Educative Task of the Catholic Community'. *Signposts and Homecomings* reviewed the principles of Catholic education and made recommendations to the Bishops' Conference.

Our Faith Story: Its Telling and Its Sharing is a different kind of book but it could only have been written on the background of *Cornerstone* and *Signposts and Homecomings.* It is a book about faith and the journey of faith by one who is a pilgrim on that journey. It is written by one who is feeling his way forward step by step alongside and with a multitude of other people who make up what we call the faith community which, however, we would hesitate to define in detail. It is a book written from within that community and has been influenced by the very many expressions of that community's self-understanding especially in the documents of the church. In the bibliography I have attempted to indicate some of the wider sources of this book; this is not easy because I have been influenced by a multiplicity of books — some of which, alas, I have long forgotten — articles too many to enumerate, lectures and perhaps most important of all, conversations with friends. This is the book's genesis which I hope roots it in the church's story, the story which goes back to the beginning, 'The Beginning of the Good News about Jesus Christ' (Mk 1:1).

I have written it for fellow pilgrims, especially for those who are in any way involved in helping other people grow in faith: parents, teachers, priests and bishops. I suppose if I attempted to describe what I do I would say I was engaged in the work of evangelisation and catechesis. I try to make my own the concern of parents helping their children grow in faith, the concern of teachers helping their pupils make sense of their lives and the concern of priests helping the community of which they are a part deepen their faith. Therefore, I am writing this book for them. It gathers together my reflections on the whole process of helping people on their faith-journey.

2. 'I'

I have been in the business of religious teaching, first as a classroom teacher and then as an adviser, for more than twenty-five years. The turmoil, the visions, the times of anguish and despair, and the hopes marking the Second Vatican Council and the years which followed are part of my own faith-journey; there is no way in which I can present my reflections except out of the context of my own life. This is the reason why you will find, and I hope not be put off by, the use of the pronoun 'I' in the pages which follow.

I am sure you dislike hearing people criticise their religious upbringing or condemn all that went on in the past. 'Today', these people say, 'things are different', and imply that everything which once took place was wrong or coloured by religious superstition. I, too, feel unhappy when I hear such remarks. I am not indulging in that kind of destructive criticism when I try to present my own story. Inevitably I will make remarks which may appear critical of the past; they are made not to comment upon the past but to show how presently held views emerged within me. This is the only way I can present the successive stages of my own faith story and my life story as a journey. What happened to me could just as easily be happening in somebody else's life today, give or take some minor details.

Perhaps only people of my own generation will be able to identify themselves with the stages or aspects of my own journey and in that sense it is obviously of limited appeal. However, I have used my own journey not so much for its own peculiar colouring and content but simply to draw your attention to your own faith-journey. You are on a journey and it is important that you should be in touch with yourself as journeying. In this way you will, in Cardinal Newman's phrase, never grow old to God.

3. Poverty, freedom and meaning

As I write, along with a multitude of other people, I am haunted by the image of the starving children of Ethiopia. It is an outrage and a blasphemy set within a world of plenty. It was the sight of such a child dying from starvation which prompted these lines to be written:

What made you old
before your years were spent?
What stretched your skin
upon your pigmy frame?
What sunk your eyes
within your skull of bone?
What drains your life
into the grave of death?

Who caused this agony, deserves to die!

And did you, God, observe it all
and stay enthroned within your hallowed sky?

'Indeed, my son,
I saw it all
and wept
with your eyes'.

The problem of poverty and hunger in some form or other affects nearly half the population of the world. It is a problem which can be solved; we have all the expertise and technology to solve it. What is lacking is the motivation.

The second problem which scars the nations of the world is totalitarianism; the domination of a people in pursuit of an ideology which ensures power, privilege and wealth to the ruling class. In such states all must submit themselves in what they do, say and even in what they think, to the mind of the state or forfeit their liberty. It is a question of freedom; there is no freedom.

Among ourselves there is a third problem, the problem of meaning. What is the meaning of life? What is life's purpose? And this leads to further questions, what does it mean to be human? and what values should govern our lives?

I am no social analyst; I do not want to pretend I have any skills in this area. All I am doing here is to describe where I am in my own reading and reflections, so that you may know the background to my writing.

What strikes me so much about today is the acquisitiveness of modern society. So much of life lies in having and possessing: and in having and possessing now! Values are interlocked with economics. Persons are worth what they make. Therefore, the elderly and the unemployed become marginal factors in society; and they for their part lose courage, lose face and lose their self-esteem. Violence in one form or another marks our relationships, and we seek ways of escape from reality through drugs and alcoholism. And all the time people genuinely ask what is the point of it all. Therefore, I want to say, if we could only solve these deep questions of our own about life's meaning we might learn how to deal with the problems of poverty and hunger and the abuse of freedom.

My faith helps me to make sense of my life: helps me to discover meaning. I suppose, therefore, the simplest description of this piece of writing is that it is about helping people make sense of life; it is about faith and how it grows and develops; it is about the values which follow from faith and how they should affect our lives and, as a result, work to make the kingdom vision of the gospel a reality in our world.

4. Ecumenism

There are many different ways of looking at ecumenical activities. Among them I have found it helpful to consider three levels of approach.

The first can be summed up in the remark, 'Some of my friends are protestant; we talk a lot about religion, occasionally we pray together; and they have been to catholic services and I have been to theirs.'

The second level is about the serious study of doctrine. Representatives of different christian churches come together to study one another's doctrinal positions, seeking for a true unity of understanding and expression without in any way compromising the truth which each one holds.

The third level is about individuals who simply look at the truth which is central to the other person's life and, foreign though it may be to their own way of thinking, nevertheless acknowledge that the God who dwells within them is also the source of that truth whereby the other lives, and hence they open themselves to hear what deep reality lies within it for themselves. I want, expressing it personally, to hear your truth, not simply its verbal expression but as it lives in you, speaking within me, within my truth.

May I draw a parallel? Many writers in recent years have discussed whether or not Jesus was political. Probably the answer to this question is that the kind of distinction we make between politics and religion was simply not valid in Jesus' time. However, the answer to the question: Did Jesus want to see Israel freed from foreign domination? is most certainly yes. Realistically, he saw there was no way in which the Jews could overthrow their enemies by force of arms; and therefore he preached 'Love your enemies', which would result in the occupying forces ceasing to be regarded as foreigners and becoming brothers; and in the Romans, too, learning how to love them. The heart of dealing with another's truth is love, which enables me to hold her/his truth within myself and not feel it as a possible source of destruction but as an enrichment.

I have not used the word 'ecumenism' in this document, but I have tried throughout to be faithful to this third level as I have just described it. Again and again, when I have spoken of our faith-journey, I have been thinking also of the multitude of people who journey with us from other christian traditions and other faiths.

5. Unity and uniformity

Take a family: father, mother, two daughters and two sons; a close-knit family, a loving family, a united family. A whole network of relationships exists. The account one son gives of what his mother means to him will be different from that of his elder sister; hers from that of her younger sister and the other brother. Each has her/his own meaning of that relationship, which in turn will be totally different from the relationship which their parents enjoy together. Different indeed, but not so different that they cannot understand one another's meaning, even though the various ways they may express their relationships differ enormously. Unity there is, but not uniformity.

We are all journeying; journeying to a God who seeks us and calls us to journey. The God we seek is a God who is inexhaustibly rich, as we discover as God reveals God's self to us in and through Jesus. Each of us is called by name to journey. We each know God in our own inner selves; each can say what God means to her/him: a vast diversity of expressions, but not so diverse that we cannot hear and understand one another. Uniformity is not the nature of the enterprise. What unites us and makes us one is the God who calls, and the trials and tribulations and the profound joy of being a journeyer and a searcher.

6. Inclusive language

There is no good reason to write a book which is entirely masculine in its language: nor, for that matter, entirely feminine. God is neither male nor female, for a start. It is not reasonable to use 'he' and 'his' rather than 'she' and 'her'; and to use 'he/she' and 'his/her' after a bit becomes very cumbersome. To avoid these problems 'inclusive language' is emerging. It involves always speaking in the plural 'they' and 'them' and not referring to God as either a 'he' or a 'she'. For the most part inclusive language flows smoothly except when a writer wants to say something like, 'God reveals himself to us'. The problem is how to avoid 'himself'. I have adopted 'God's self'; so that sentence reads, 'God reveals God's self to us'. You may find this somewhat annoying at first but I think you will get used to it.

Part One

Telling Our Faith Story

1

Making a Start

1. Kinds of Question

Dear Sir,
Once upon a time, when I was young, being a Catholic was pretty straightforward. You said your prayers, went to Mass on Sundays, did not eat meat on Fridays, went to confession, and you believed what the church told you to believe; and, may I add, you had a healthy respect for God. Now I do not know where I am. All right, I may be oversimplifying things the way I put it, but a lot of my friends agree with me. We all like a lot of things in what we call the new-look church, but really what's it all about? We are specially worried about our children and what we are to tell them. I wish somebody would spell it out for me. Perhaps he would tell me what he believes, to see if it makes any sense to me and my friends.

Yours sincerely,

Anxious and Bemused

I could begin this book 'Dear Anxious and Bemused', and respond to the writer's request by spelling out what I believe, hoping that it would make sense to Mr/Mrs/Miss Anxious and Bemused. However, at first sight, at least, an account of what I believe hardly meets another request I have received from elsewhere, which is to produce a document about how one generation passes on its religious heritage to the next, and in particular how one generation helps its young to believe the truths it received from its parents and grandparents. You may think at this point, with some justification that it is not a little presumptuous of me to have accepted this brief: do not feel bad about that thought — you are right! Nevertheless, as I reflect, I realise this 'handing on' belongs to the whole generation: you and I, all of us, have a part

25

to play in it. And so for what it's worth I set myself to offer my reflections on this subject.

I owe a great deal of my present religious understanding of life to those people who were responsible for producing the famous penny catechism: not just to the catechism itself, but even more to the influence it had on the faith of the generation which formed me. That catechism has had enormous influence on the religious heritage of our country, and still has. The questions and answers (with their notes) still echo in my mind, though I am no longer word-perfect by any means. They weave in and out of new answers which, I believe, are new ways of looking at and thinking about old truths: new ways which are the fruit of the Second Vatican Council and of my own experience of life, and which have in time provoked new questions to keep me searching. And so as I reflect on what I have been asked to do in this book I come to realise that I have already been caught up in its subject, the handing on the faith to another generation: that though the prospect of answering 'Dear Anxious and Bemused' may be somewhat daunting, it is not as presumptuous as it may appear at first sight. I have lived through the tumultuous and turbulent years following the Second Vatican Council; I have been trying to make its emerging teaching my own; I have tried to live in its spirit and help others to do likewise; and at the same time I have attempted to integrate the Church's now with her past: tried to understand and present her life and teaching, as it is now developing, as one piece with the story I received as a child; the story which goes back to the beginning and which we believe to be true because God promised that the Holy Spirit would never desert our people, because God is faithful.

2. Story

And so, dear Anxious and Bemused, I shall tell you what I believe: I hope it will make sense to you.

I am going to tell you my story and I hope that my story finds echoes in your own life, and that my story meets strands of your own story. I fear you may already be getting somewhat impatient with my use of the word, 'story'. I can hear you say, 'What I want are facts, not stories!' Once I thought that religious truths were great statements dropped from heaven into the minds of humankind labelled 'You shall believe!' and, because they had such obvious divine origins, I believed: I accepted them as truths.

There were very many such beliefs: God is the creator, God is infinite in all perfections, Jesus is God's Son, the Holy Spirit is the Third Person of the Blessed Trinity, and so on. Where indeed did they all come from? I was taught, for example, that Jesus Christ rose from the dead: I learnt to believe this. Well, if Jesus did rise from the dead, somebody must have seen him alive after he had died. Mary Magdalene, for one: she ran to the apostles and said: 'I've seen the Lord!' and told them her story; and Peter saw the Lord and told his story; so did Thomas; so did the couple on their way to Emmaus. Each told a story of how each had seen the risen Lord. The stories added up and began to be told and eventually they came to be written down. And people of succeeding generations read the accounts and found that what they read there tallied with their own experience and they too could say 'We've seen the Lord', and tell their story.

When, therefore, I begin to write to you in order to give an account of what I believe, I enter the world of story. Luke at the beginning of his gospel writes: 'I in my turn, after carefully going over the whole story from the beginning, have decided to write an ordered account for you, Theophilus . . .' (1:3). A wise person once wrote, 'Believe the story, not the teller of the story.' Now the point I am making is this: I write to you, Anxious and Bemused, with no credentials; I am not asking you to believe me, I want you to listen to the story I tell. If it is a good story you will recognise the truth of it because it will echo within your own experience: you will say, 'That's what I feel!' 'That makes sense!' And where and when this does not happen, you must share your experience with me, because together we are trying to tell one story about a God whom we have made our own and who has made us God's people.

3. Religion and life

In my childhood I was well instructed in my religion. I was taught about the Mass and how to take part in it, how to pray, how to honour the saints, how to go to confession, the importance of self-denial. I was taught that my religion was the most important thing in my life; that I should be proud to be a catholic; that I should never forsake my religion even if it meant dying for it, like my catholic forbears. Now even as I write I believe I am beginning to uncover the weakness in my religious upbringing; it was all about *having* the true religion.

You know the phrase 'the religious dimension of life', meaning life divided into watertight compartments. Well, that in a nutshell was where the weakness lay. My religion was a dimension of life — a compartment of my life: it was not integrated with the whole of my life, in spite of the fact that my teachers did their best to show me how my religion should influence everything I did and said and thought. In fact, they taught me to say at the beginning of each day the Morning Offering which emphasised that my day did belong to God and that God was to be found in every moment of it; but somehow or other the religious understanding on which the Morning Offering was based never really affected me. For me, religion remained a facet of life, albeit the most important facet. And I think the reason why this happened lay in the kind of God who was presented to me for my worship and service. I had perhaps a too healthy respect for this God!

I learnt that 'God made me to know him, love him and serve him in this world and be happy with him forever in the next'; that 'God is a Supreme Being who alone exists of himself and is infinite in all perfections'. I could easily understand the need to go to church to worship such a God, to make every effort to obey this God under whose all-seeing eye I spent every moment of my life, and the need I had to beg God's pardon when I broke one of the divine laws; and I was ready to accept that God would reward me for being good and punish me for being bad. All this I could understand; it was all so logical. What I could not grasp was how such a God could be part and parcel of my everyday life; I could not make this God part of my feeling life. God was much too remote, away in the heavens. In fact, to be perfectly honest, I wanted to keep this God at arm's length.

4. The same God but different!

So what happened to me was that I felt my way into a new image of God. I say 'feel' advisedly, because intellectually I was not acquiring new facts about God. What was happening to me was that the old truths began to take shape within me in a new way; they gradually became meaningful to me in a way they had never done before.

This took place because the context of my life changed. I had always lived in a highly authoritarian structure, both within my own family and within the religious life which I had entered. This authoritarianism reinforced my concept of God: my parents, my teachers, my first confession priest, my religious superiors were all God-figures in my life and I regarded them all with a sense of awe and fear, no matter how much at another level I knew they loved me. Now this began to change, and I felt free for the first time in my life to begin to reshape my image of God.[1]

It would take too long to recount the stages of this reshaping but suddenly, almost without warning, the bible began to speak to me.[2]

> Do not be afraid for I have redeemed you:
> I have called you by your name: you are mine.
>
> (Isaiah 43:1)
>
> See, I have branded you on the palms of my hands.
>
> (Isaiah 49:16)
>
> I was like someone who lifts an infant close against his cheek.
>
> (Hosea 11:4)

The realisation came that this biblical God was my God; and the one this God was calling by name was me. I was branded on God's hands. When Jesus called out to his listeners to address Yahweh God as 'Abba'! (the child's daddy!) he was telling me how to approach the God who was infinite in all perfections. I was to understand the definition of God as one who made me to know him, love him and serve him in this world and to be happy with him in the next very differently. Does a mother give birth to a child *in order* that that child should know, love and serve her? She wants the child to love her, but first she gives

---

[1] I do not want to make this document too personal, but if it is to find echoes in the reader's own life something of my own story is relevant. My entry into religious life (Society of Jesus) reinforced the image of God I had built for myself. Along with all forms of religious life at that time, the Jesuits were authoritarian and they specialised in obedience. If my memory serves me well, we were never directly encouraged to read the bible, not even the new testament; whereas time was specifically allocated to certain spiritual writers renowned for their views on religious discipline.

[2] This happened some ten years after my ordination: after twenty-four years of religious life.

herself with love to her child. She shares herself with her child. God 'breathed into his nostrils a breath of life and this man became a living being' (Genesis 2:7), and thus God who is love communicated the very essence of God's self to the work of God's hands. God loved me into existence and made me capable of loving.

I had been brought up to think of God as some remote and powerful figure who looked down upon the human race from a throne above the heavens: 'Far away, sad at heart, I call to you' (Ps 61:2). I had to get up and go to God: 'I will go to the altar of God' *(Introibo ad altare Deum)*. Now I was coming to understand that I did not have to get up and go to God, that God is totally involved in my life and in the lives of everybody I daily meet.

I find it very hard to put all this into words. At school I had learnt to prove the existence of God; we used the language of philosophy: we proved that, because things moved, ultimately there must be some thing, some power, someone who is responsible for all movement, who is not moved by someone else, who is called the Unmoved Mover; that this someone is also the First Cause of an almost (but not quite) endless chain of causes going back to the beginning — to this someone. Everybody and everything, moreover, is wearing out; the human body declines, grows weaker and dies; so too does nature; even the mighty hills are eroded by the weather. All this argued for someone who is not subject to such a process: we called this one the Necessary Being. God is indeed all this: God is the source of all that I can see, know and feel.

> The night-sky proclaims God's glory,
> the day-sky, his creative skill;
> day after day, this is re-attested,
> night after night, this is reaffirmed.
> (Ps 19:1-2)

But God is also deep within the work of God's hands, within every human being on the face of the earth as creative love, whether that person acknowledges God or not. A mother loving the baby at her breast is loving her baby with God's love; husbands give God's love to their wives, wives to their husbands. God is not simply the cause of this loving, but somehow or other we have to go even further and say that God is in the loving itself: God is Love. God is the relationship: God is the forgiveness which my friend offers me after I have hurt him; God is the beauty I see, the joy I experience, the helping hand I am offered, the patience and the sympathy I receive from people, the wonder I feel at the world's marvels, and even in the sadness I experience at its folly. God is each of these things and yet God is much more. God is within my imagination; within the thought-patterns my mind conceives; within my dreams and desires; within my experiences, giving them depth and meaning; dwelling within me, not simply to keep me in existence, but to enable me to become the kind of person the Divine Goodness has in mind for me. In an extraordinary way (and I hesitate to put it this way because of how audacious it sounds) God wants to be fully God within me — within me as this particular human being. As I struggle to be what God wants me to be or, more accurately, as I struggle to respond to God's love creating me, so is God struggling within my struggling to be God's self within me. The breath-taking truth about this whole business is God's great delight and longing to be totally involved in it, 'delighting to be with the sons of men' (Proverbs 8:31). God, says that strange prophet Zephaniah, 'will dance with shouts of joy for you as on a day of festival' (Zephaniah 3:17).

I began to see too that God's presence and activity in this world, and in the lives of people, does not depend on its being acknowledged by believers. God is not believed into existence. John, my friend, did not believe in God; he was an atheist: and yet God was no less in him than in me. I was aware how much he loved his wife, Irene, who likewise did not believe in God; how rich and loving was their family life. I became aware of God at work not only in individuals but also in groups, in communities, in societies and in nations; in the struggles of governments to care for their peoples; in the endeavours of organisations to feed hungry peoples; in the striving of the oppressed for freedom; in the search for peace among enemies and in the claims of minority groups for their rights.

This I slowly discovered: that the God for whom I had such a healthy respect in my childhood was, after all, no remote deity sitting unmoved in the distant heavens, but was immediately involved in my life and in the lives of all the people around me. Scripture cried out that

God had compassion on the human race and entered into its sorrows and joys:

> Your creator will be your husband.   (Isaiah 54:5)

> I will betroth you to myself forever,
> betroth you with integrity and justice,
> with tenderness and love:
> I will betroth you to myself with faithfulness
> and you will come to know Yahweh.
> (Hosea 1:19-22)

Now I could begin to live with this God. On the one hand there was no doubt that God, this God, is the all-powerful, ever-living One, infinite in all perfections, the Supreme Being who controls the universe, the Lord of the living and the dead; yet, on the other hand, this God is the God of tenderness and compassion who 'lured me and led me into the wilderness and there had spoken to my heart' (Hosea 2:16).

5. The darkness of sin

In coming to realise more clearly God's presence and saving activity in the life of every human being on the face of the earth, I was being continually questioned by the presence and activity of evil; evil not just within myself but deep within the lives of everybody; within the very structure of the society of which I was a member and within the relationships between races and nations. Hatred and division permeated the human race.

For my own part I made St Paul's words my own: 'I fail to carry out the things I want to do, and I find myself doing the things I hate' (Romans 7:15). For me sin was offending God by breaking the divine law: God was the law-giver. Frequent confession was the remedy for my guilt: it restored the peace I lost by my sinning, made God my friend again.

Then there took place a conversion, best summed up perhaps in the words of a friend of mine who had undergone a similar experience:

> 'For the first thirty-odd years of my life,' he said, 'I was terrified of God. Again and again I felt that I had been damned; and justly damned. How often I went to confession to sort myself out with

God; there I was truly sorry, made a good resolution which lasted but a short time and then I sinned again and once more incurred the divine wrath. Here was I, basically a good person, so I thought myself, deliberately giving in to my human weakness and breaking the law. It was somewhere within this understanding of myself that my conversion occurred. I realised that I was not basically a good person who sinned, but a sinner who occasionally did good, and that the very good I did was not the result of my own unaided effort but was itself the gift of God: my goodness was God working in me. And thus I came to the stunning realisation that God loved me, a sinner. It was all very well to have always believed that God loves the sinner and hates sin: this was a nice theory until I knew myself to be the sinner.'

I suppose the next piece to fall into place was the nature of God's love for me: God's love is life-giving; it is creative. God is loving me into the fullness of life; or put it this way: God is loving me into being, into becoming what God wants me to be, which is to be fully and completely human. Now I came to see sin in terms of relationships: by sinning I turned away from God's never-ceasing creative love for me; by sinning I turned away from what God wanted me to be: I nurtured what was inhuman in myself. This completely gave the lie to that phrase which some people use to excuse wrongdoing: 'After all, I'm only human!' It is the human that is good, to which we are all called to aspire — the work of creative love; evil is inhuman.

Of course, one can define sin as breaking the law[3] but the malice of sin lies in the harm and the hurt it does at a personal level, at the level of one's relationships to one's fellow human beings and to God; because the love of God and the love of people is one love. To sin against a human being, to bring unhappiness deliberately into the life of another person, is to sin against God, whether or not the sinner acknowledges God as the source and origin of humankind. To foster what is inhuman is to disfigure and distort God's creative design.

So, slowly, my own understanding of sin evolved, and this brought about a change in the way I thought about the world and the society of

[3] The Ten Commandments are one answer to the question 'What does it mean to be a human being?', given to a people who had been rescued from slavery.

which I was a part. This is not the place to preach sermons or to mora-lise: all I am trying to do is to say something about my own faith-jour-ney. Now, I suppose, I am trying to become more sensitive to every-thing that depersonalises a human being: about everything which makes individuals less human — that lessens their value and worth. I am becoming aware of deep-rooted thought-patterns and attitudes in myself which can lead to depersonalisation, and I see the same patterns in society and in nations: the many 'isms' which reduce and belittle the human person to the level of a thing. How deeply I am affected by that ethic which values people by their success! How society belittles indi-viduals by allowing unemployment to accelerate without preparing people for alternative ways of living! How nations use various kinds of oppression and torture to subdue whole peoples to live under a parti-cular political hierarchy!

6. A God for daily life

The problem or the weakness of my own religious education, there-fore, was not in its presentation of doctrine (this was true to its day), nor with the encouragement I received to be faithful to the practices of my religion (albeit with the stick of mortal sin!), but in how to relate religion to life. I have been arguing that the kind of God who was pre-sented to me was not the kind of God I could make part of my daily life, and therefore my religious education created a religious sphere, a reli-gious layer, which was very difficult to integrate with the rest of my life. It produced a holy world into which I had to make a very explicit and conscious effort to enter.

For me, the way to integration has been through a new understand-ing of God: of a God who does not stand over my life as a threat or a source of continual guilt, but one who is totally involved with my bumbling attempts to be a human being; one who has compassion on my selfishness, puts up with my opinionated self, is patient with my dark desires and fantasies and still keeps on loving me into the fullness of being which the divine goodness designs for me — which is to become completely human. I can live with such a God. I do not have to step out of my ordinary world to discover this God. Clearly I am struggling to understand this more clearly; I am feeling my way for-ward. 'I am still running, trying to capture the prize for which Christ Jesus captured me' (Philippians 3:12.)

2

The Journey

1. Travelling

You see, without any effort we have arrived at the concept of life as a journey. I know this is not an original idea. It is one of the basic themes of the bible: from the call to Abraham to leave his own home and set off for a place which God would show him, to Israel's wanderings in the desert, to Christ's own journey to Jerusalem and to St Augustine's 'the church, like a pilgrim in a foreign land, presses forward amid the persecutions of the world and the consolations of God' (quoted in *Lumen Gentium 8*). My own feeling about this journey image is that while we accept it, we do not fully appreciate its implications for our ordinary lives. We are on a journey to God: we have not reached our goal. We are in the process of becoming: we have not yet become what we are called to be. 'Be perfect just as your heavenly Father is perfect' (Matthew 5:48) exhorts us to receive the gift of becoming completely human which God holds out to us as we travel on. Keeping the commandments perfectly, and living within the spirit of the Beatitudes completely, is part of the ideal state towards which we are making our way: we are not there yet!

I have just been speaking about how God is present to every human being on the face of the earth, not simply keeping each one in existence, but drawing each one into union with God's self; in fact, God yearns and longs to disclose God's self deep within the being of each person: 'Look I am standing at the door knocking' (Revelation 3:20). God calls everybody to discover the divine goodness within themselves. The journey of which I speak is not a journey out beyond human existence but a journey within, into the very components of life itself, to the Ground of our being.

The other side of this picture is how human beings respond to God's desire to disclose the divine self. Some, deeply buried in the darkness of materialism and self-centredness, barely respond at all; some, because early experiences have distorted values, hesitate; some have so disfigured a concept of God that they view God as cruel and heartless and find it difficult to begin; some are terrified of God; some have enormous problems with every kind of relationship and tremble to become involved; some, because of personal weakness of which they are ashamed, do not want God to come too close; some, struggling with the messiness of human existence and how to live according to gospel values, welcome God. However, God is calling each one and is at work within the life of each. And each one can come to know the truth of St Augustine's exclamation after his conversion: 'You, my God, were there all the time and I did not know you.'

2. A travelling faith

I must admit that I came upon the idea of the faith-journey late in life. In my own religious upbringing, faith was something you received *en bloc* as it were. Faith was simply a series of beliefs: the trinity, the incarnation, the redemption, etc. as laid down in one of the creeds. I believed without doubting the mysterious truths of the creeds revealed by God. I had the faith. I knew it was possible to lose it. In my childhood my teachers spoke of people losing the faith: they lost it because they had not been faithful to their religious duties. It was difficult to get back! It was only when I began to distinguish beliefs from faith that I began to make sense in a new way of many things in my religion. I came to use 'faith' as the word to describe our relationship to God: 'I put my faith in you.' Faith involves trust and love. The latin words *Credo in unum Deum* mean, 'I place or put my heart in God, in God who loves me'. Faith is the relationship, the incredible, tender love of God for me, and my tentative response. Beliefs describe the relationship: they attempt to put into words what faith is, so that I can share my faith with others. Beliefs try to say who God is for us, how God acts in the world and what it means to belong to God. Inevitably beliefs will always limp: it is impossible to express fully in human language exactly the truth about God and God's involvement with humankind. We are always trying to penetrate more deeply these truths, and hence we are always trying to refine the way we express our beliefs. We are ever trying to understand the trinity, creation, incarnation, redemption, etc: there is a mysterious depth about each of these truths and, though we can know something about each, we shall never know everything.

3. Faith and conversion

And so at last I came to see faith in terms of personal relationships: between myself and God, and between myself and my fellow human beings in whom God dwelt, but it took me even longer to see the link between how this relationship could develop and deepen and the whole idea of conversion. Yet once glimpsed it was so very obvious. God is love dwelling within the depths of my being from the first moment of my existence, and ever offering to share God's self with me in companionship. And this love was life-giving: it was life itself. The one who espouses and nourishes the true life espouses and nourishes love. The problem of the faith-relationship lay not in God but in me. God offers life in all its fullness: the divine life which is love. God, however, does not force God's self on me. The very nature of a personal relationship requires a free response: and there is so much in myself which shies from embracing life in all its richness. My selfishness mars my self-giving; my blurred vision fails to recognise the truth; my fear undermines my ability to trust the goodness I encounter; and yet, as scripture recounts, God waits patiently in every moment of my life, at every twist and turn of the journey, offering me the opportunity to live life to the full. God dwells within the multitudinous experiences of growing up, maturing, falling in love, settling down, working, recreating; in happiness, in sorrow, in health, in sickness, in success, in failure, in disappointment, in growing old, in dying; offering me a way to enter more deeply into life, to penetrate more profoundly its meaning. And each time I make a choice for what is more fully human I allow God's love to touch me and I respond to life. I yield a little selfishness, see a little clearer, trust a little more, so I journey on: God's love has worked a conversion (albeit very small) in me. Conversion is all about taking little steps towards becoming more and more human, according to God's understanding of human.

Jesus came preaching, crying: 'The Kingdom of God is at hand.

Repent and believe the Good News' (Mark 1:15). He was calling out to each of his listeners to change: to be converted. The history of all religions tells of great and dramatic conversions, but all conversions are not traumatic. Jesus' call is for each one of us to opt for life and for everything that is life-giving, for truth, justice, love, peace, courage, friendship, community; and each option is a conversion and conversions move the faith-journey onwards.

4. Faith and meaning

Here I want to underline something which has been spoken of countless times. Again and again people speak of the meaninglessness of life, of the pointlessness of so much of modern existence. The number of suicides, the prevalence of drugs, the alarming degree of violence all speak of a massive inability to enjoy life, of a sad joylessness.

Nevertheless, everybody has some reason for continuing to stay alive, albeit a very thin one, perhaps the fear of dying. Now in this broadest sense we can say that everybody has faith because everybody manages to find some meaning in life; though by faith I do not necessarily mean religious faith. However, it is out of the way that people make sense of their lives that faith can grow and develop, and perhaps come to receive and accept the gospel. Hence it is extremely important to see the necessity of helping people simply to find meaning for their own lives. I see that my own faith not only attempts to answer questions about the mysteries of human existence but also to illuminate the richness of human life: what it means to be alive.

5. Faith and religion

Faith is the relationship; beliefs describe the relationship. There is the closest connection between faith and beliefs because as soon as I begin to think and speak of who God is for me, I use images, ideas and words which are the makings of beliefs. And these images, ideas and words I have learnt from the human family to which I belong. It may well be that these ways of expressing what my faith means to me are inadequate: they only approximate to what I feel. Often we have heard people say, 'How difficult it is for me to put into words what I feel!' Yet this is the only way we have of sharing what is deepest and most important to us. All of this leads us to define religion as a system of shared beliefs and the values which are implicit in them.

I could leave it at this for the moment as far as our present discussion is concerned, but for completeness I would like to add a further word about the definition of religion as a system of beliefs and values. This definition is very broad and it includes ways of living and believing which do not include belief in God: Marxism, for example. Where God is at the heart of people's lives and beliefs, the way they worship God and the way they should behave become important in the description of religion: hence, the description of a religion centred upon God must include creed (beliefs), code (rules governing behaviour) and cult (ways of worship).

6. The Pilgrimage

There is nothing very neat and tidy about our pilgrimage. Every human being is called to journey; everyone is on the pilgrimage since everyone is in the process of becoming what God has designed for each one to become: to enjoy life to the full, to be as fully human as possible; but not everyone is at the same point in the journey. There are those who, on the one hand, consider it wishful thinking to believe in anything which is not immediately evident to their senses and are struggling with the whole idea of God, those who are trying to free themselves from superstitions, and those who are trying to trust: while, on the other hand, there are those who are giving up everything to go and serve the poor, those who are being more and more attracted by prayer and those who are finding God in their own experience of pain and disability. Take any group of people — there you will find individuals at all sorts of points on the journey. I know I can stand up and profess my faith with the community at eucharist and yet find myself acting, out of completely secular and unchristian[4] values on many an occasion. Again, I can profess with my lips a particular belief yet be very unsure of what it really means; and still further I know that

[4] Unchristian or secular values: one has to be careful how one uses the word 'secular'. Secular simply means what belongs to the world, and the world belongs to God: it is good. However there is a use of the word which means the opposite: in this sense secularism//secularist means a world which organises itself specifically without God.

if I canvassed the congregation about what each understood by a particular belief I would get many different answers.

As I came to reflect on the faith-journey and about the diversity of faith even within a given church community, I knew I was beginning to enter the world of pluralism and the problems this creates for many people. It is too easy to say that everybody should believe the same thing and expect everybody to do so: we can all be saying the same words, as we've seen, yet understanding them in very different ways, simply because our powers of understanding are so different. At the faith level of relationship there can be an even greater diversity. A mother loves all her children, but with each one she has a unique relationship: each child may speak of what her/his mother means to her/him and the other children will recognise something of their own relationship in what is said, but know too there is something missing which is theirs and theirs alone.

Pluralism has always been a factor of faith and believing. What then are we to say of the one faith to which we are called? or of the one building of which we are part? or of 'All of you are one in Christ Jesus'? (Galatians 3:28). Pluralism does not disrupt unity and it does not demand uniformity. Our oneness in faith arises from our journeying together in response to the call of the one living God. Our unity in believing is attested by our genuine desire to understand our faith in the light of the faith story we have received from our forebears and in our desire to express it as clearly as possible in our own culture. We have, therefore, to learn to live with people whose beliefs may be very different from our own, respecting that they too are on their faith-journey. Unity in diversity comes about when each person sincerely attempts to discover the other person's truth and tries to make it her/his own and, in the process, looks beyond to a further and deeper truth which contains the essence of both and yet moves on into new reaches of truth.

7. Faith and education

Perhaps it would be useful here for me to summarise a number of points which I find important:

a. The heart of faith is the relationship between myself and God and other people: it is commitment.

b. Life is a journey of faith in that it is the continuing attempt to deepen this commitment, the continuing struggle to discover God in the depths of one's own life and in the life of everyone. Deepening this commitment means opting for life and for everything that is life-giving.

c. Faith helps me to make sense of my own life and the world in which I live. Faith gives meaning to human existence. Everybody, therefore, who continues to find some reason for living has faith, in this very broad understanding of faith. By faith here I do not necessarily mean religious faith. Nevertheless, this faith-meaning is very important to the journey.

d. Therefore, when we come to examine where people are on the faith-journey, we discover people at all sorts of different places; some struggling to begin, others pressing on. All I am doing here is to emphasise the respect we need to give to the faith of every person. We all need to feel we are accepted and affirmed in the endeavours we make to journey through life, and to feel there is nothing wrong in being where we are. On the one hand we do not want to be made feel guilty, yet on the other hand we need support to journey on. One of the most important factors in the support we need to offer each other is affirmation. By affirmation I mean helping each other understand more clearly what gives meaning to our lives and what are the values which govern them. By helping each other understand what actually gives meaning to our lives, we are preparing each other to deepen that meaning. To those who have no particular religious meaning, we offer the meaning which emerges from our Christian story (our tradition), so that they may examine their meaning in its light and be challenged by the implications of the Good News. In the past, instead of trying to discover the meaning which people give to their lives and building on that, we have tended to disregard their meaning and simply offered a worked-out religious faith to take its place. It seems to me that we must give much more time and effort to helping people come to terms with the need to search for meaning so that, if the Christian story does not touch them, at least they will continue the search for a meaning to their lives.

e. Beliefs describe the commitment to God. They are attempts to put into human language what is my relationship to God and in consequence to everybody and everything else, in order to be able to share my faith with others.

f. Religion is a shared system of beliefs. Religion is frequently described in terms of creed, code and cult.

g. Christian beliefs, ways of living and behaving, and ways of worship began to take shape as those who had seen the risen Christ started to tell their story: 'We've seen the Lord!' This was the work of the Holy Spirit: the gift promised by Jesus. It was the Holy Spirit who brought the church into being and who forever remains the Teller of the christian story.

h. The story has continued to be handed on generation after generation, each generation making it its own, putting its stamp on it, telling it in a way which meets the cultural and religious needs of its day.

i. As the church developed so did its structure, a hierarchical structure. Within this structure the pope and bishops have the special task of Keepers of the story. Theirs is the special responsibility of keeping the story true to its origins.

3

The Church

1. Ways of looking at the church

In the last section I referred to the community story; now I want to develop some thoughts about the community, the Catholic Church. When I was being given my own religious education the church came across to me chiefly as the pope, the bishops and the priests: the church was the 'perfect society' to which one was privileged to belong. More than anything else I learnt to respect and obey those who had authority from God, namely, the pope, the bishops and the priests. At that time the laity, in the way we use that word today, were hardly ever mentioned at all.

Considerable emphasis was placed on the idea of the church as the One Ark of Salvation, as light in a world of darkness, and as the guardian of the deposit of truth: and I suppose I thought of her more than anything else in terms of the sacraments. Suffice it to say she appeared to me first and foremost as a rock-like and paternalistic institution.

During the last twenty years, since the Second Vatican Council, I have lived through a revolution. The Council has enriched my understanding of the church immeasurably. It has thrown new light on the religious knowledge I received in my younger days, and it has helped me to see that there are very many different ways of looking at the church.

Take 'authority' as an example. As I noted above, I thought of the pope, bishops and priests as having a very special relationship to God which resulted in their having specialised knowledge, and endowed them with power and authority over the members of the church who were their subjects. The role of the subjects was to obey, and in obeying they submitted to the will of God. This kind of authority puts the emphasis on order, and on moulding the subjects to fit into a well-tried way of life which had been led by generation after generation and which enshrined God's eternal truths; a way of life, changeless in a world of change, was characteristic of the church as the perfect society and possessed something of the timeless nature of God.

However, there is another way of looking at authority which takes into account not only the presence of God's Spirit in those who 'have authority', pope, bishops and priests, but also in the subjects. In this understanding, the bishop, for example, sees himself as discovering the will of God with his subjects. Bishop and subjects listen to each other and pray together as a way of finding the way forward together.

Now both these kinds of authority throw important light upon what happens within the life of the church. The former's emphasis on handing on a traditional body of truth and way of life is crucial. Today, as much as at any time, we need the assurance that we are true to what God revealed of the divine selfhood in Jesus Christ, and that the values which Jesus lived and died for are still our values. We need to know that our story is one and the same story as that told by the apostles; but equally important is the other view of authority with its emphasis on the presence and activity of the Holy Spirit within every single person who makes up the church. The laity are no less important than the clergy. Lay men and women do not just 'belong' to the church, they are as much church as the pope, the bishops and the priests. And the emphasis on the presence of the Holy Spirit points to a dynamic living quality in the church which was not evident in the fortress image of the former approach to authority. This renewed understanding and emphasis on the activity of the Holy Spirit enables the church to handle the divine revelation committed to her, not simply as a static deposit, but as a living entity in which her members are continually seeing old truths in a new light and new truths evolving in the light of the old. This indeed is responding to the words of Jesus, 'If you make my word your home, you will indeed be my disciples', i.e. if you live within my revelation, 'you will learn the truth and the truth will make you free' (John 8:31-32). And 'every scribe who becomes a disciple of the kingdom of heaven is like a householder who brings out from his storeroom things both new and old' (Matthew 14:51-52). It is the householder who is the Teller of the story, the Holy Spirit.

Perhaps, I need to add a word of qualification lest I give the impression that this newer approach to authority is already firmly established in the church. I am not saying that! What I am saying is that this approach to authority has been emerging in the church as a result of the thinking about the church stimulated by the Vatican Council. There is still a long way to go for it to be universally accepted and implemented. Much work needs doing in order to make it a reality.

Some people name this authority as the authority of service and see it as a characteristic of the church as servant. This idea of the church as servant brings us into the whole field of different models of the church. I was brought up in a church in which the word 'model' was not used but, if we were to apply it to the church of my youth, we might call that church the institutional church, as many writers do. However, there is a flaw in simply calling it 'institutional', because every model of the church must have some structure and therefore some institutional elements. Perhaps, because of its emphasis on tradition and authority, it would be better to call it patriarchical.

I find the idea of models of the church helpful. Models are ways in which the church is church. Take, for example, the education of small children: one way of educating them would be to put them all in the classroom seated in orderly fashion in desks before a teacher who gives them lessons; another way would be to teach them according to some method which emphasised the children's participation: and yet another would be the approach of the nanny-governess, once used in richer victorian houses. So we have three models of educating small children. In each model an education is being given rightly and properly and yet each model has its own character, structure, approach and method. Similarly, the different models of the church speak of the great diversity of the church and at the same time relate and inter-relate with one another, while in no way undermining her unity. There are many models of the church, each with its own characteristics and structure: here I would like to speak of four which are in frequent use.

The servant church: this model takes its inspiration from Jesus who came to us as one who serves: 'Here am I among you as one who serves' (Luke 22:27).

The church as herald: this model lays emphasis on the church's task of proclaiming the good news to the nations: 'Go, therefore, make disciples of all nations' (Matthew 28:19).

The church as prophet: the prophet is not so much involved with the future as in pointing out where God is in the present: the church acts as prophet in reading the signs of the times in making humankind aware of how and where God acts in the world.

The church as community: the church is called to be a sign of the unity to which God calls every human being on the face of the earth: 'May they all be one, Father, may they be one in us' (John 17:21). God desires that we should all live together in truth, justice, peace and love. The eucharist is both the sign of the community and the means of achieving it.

2. The church and the mission of Christ

I have been presenting a view of church which certainly does not correspond to the experience of church which I had in my own childhood, nor perhaps even to much of my present experience. That past experience presented a church which was very holy and very religious in the narrow sense of these words. The idea that the church existed to set human beings free from everything that held them captive, from selfishness, superstition, fear, power which uses people as things, etc. in order that they should enjoy being human beings, certainly never appeared in the religious education text books which I had in my school desk — rather the church, to my childish mind, was the unique 'spoilsport' which at every opportunity said 'No'.

The church came across to me in this way because she had, especially during the nineteenth century, to defend herself against those who accused her of holding teachings which were against reason; therefore, she developed very strong rational arguments to defend herself. As a result of this defence, the church tended to present a view of God which emphasised God's otherness, God's power, God's infinite perfections, God's changelessness, God's authority. This, however, had great difficulty in coping with and expressing God's involvement in the sheer messiness of human existence. This image of God was moreover quite clearly male, presented by a highly masculine church. Granted this kind of God, a rigid legal system emerged: God was after all the Divine Lawgiver. Sin was breaking one of God's laws, and the seriousness of the sin depended on the importance of the law. The doctrinal teaching was fixed, firm and final, handed down from one generation to the next with no deviations, because it was God's revelation given absolutely once and for all through Jesus Christ. And it was, therefore, in no way surprising that the kind of worship which emerged from this notion of God was formalistic, rigid, unbending and impersonal. What other way could one worship the First Cause, the Prime Mover and Supreme Creator?

Further, the way in which Jesus was presented to me put no emphasis on his humanity. The expected answer to the classroom question, 'Who is Jesus?' was, 'Jesus is God'. It was thought that unless one especially emphasised his divinity one was belittling him! The problem was, and always will be, how to cope with Jesus in his rich reality. However, today I believe we have found a way of speaking about Jesus which enables us, to a much greater extent than say fifty years ago, to identify ourselves with him and at the same time not to minimise his divinity. As we rethink ourselves into God's nearness, so we get in touch with the humanity of Jesus; and it is out of this understanding of Jesus that our concept of church emerges.

The relationship of Jesus to the church is fundamental. The church is Christ in our world, not to condemn it but to save it; so the church is sent and exists in the world for the world's salvation. The church strives to continue Christ's saving mission:

> The spirit of the Lord has been given to me
> for he has anointed me.
> He has anointed me to bring good news to the poor,
> to proclaim liberty to captives
> and to the blind new sight,
> to set the downtrodden free,
> to proclaim the Lord's year of favour.
>
> (Luke 4:18-19)

3. The community which serves

I would now like to develop this picture of the church, which I feel is being demanded by the times in which we are living.

Jesus comes into the world as one 'sent' by God, not to condemn the world but to save it, to recreate and transform it according to the design God has for it. Jesus does this through a life of service. One of his great qualities was his power of compassion, his ability to enter into the problems and sufferings of others and make them his own. St Luke says of the good Samaritan that he was moved by compassion (Luke 10:33) meaning, literally, his heart was melting within him at the sight of the wounded man. It was thus that Jesus entered into the lives of the people he met. He became the good Samaritan to each of them, helping them to discover meaning in their lives, offering ways of transforming their hatred into love, of mending their quarrels, of enlightening their ignorance, of removing barriers to hearing God's call, of bringing joy to those in despair, of helping people love the truth, of making people see that pride, hypocrisy, jealousy, greed, were denials of life. He was indeed life-giving: 'I have come that they may have life and have it to the full' (John 10:20).

Jesus offered hope: he preached a future. He spoke of a kingdom belonging to God, the beginnings of which God had commissioned him to establish and which would reach its fullness only in the very self of God. He took up the language of the prophets to describe this kingdom in which all men, women, and children would live together in peace, truth, justice and charity, sharing the world's goods which God was giving them. The prophets used metaphors to describe this kingdom: they spoke of a land flowing with milk and honey, of the lion asleep with the lamb, of the infant playing over the cobra's hole. Jesus used parables: the kingdom was like a wedding banquet, a pearl of great price, a treasure hidden in a field, a city on a hill. Jesus was a man who lived and worked and died for a vision of new life, a vision endorsed by resurrection.

It is this picture of Jesus which leads me to construct my image of the kind of church needed by the society in which I live. Therefore, I see the church as that community which follows Jesus and struggles to make his transforming mission her own. The church is part of the society which she is striving to renew in the light of the teaching and values of the gospel, in response to Christ's mandatum: 'I give you a new commandment: love one another; just as I have loved you, you also must love one another' (John 13:34).

The ordained ministry is called to serve the community by celebrating sacramentally the daily experiences of people who are trying to live out the gospel. As the members of the community struggle to offer healing, forgiveness, unity, peace and love in their daily lives: so the ordained ministry leads them to celebrate their daily lives sacramentally, so that they may come to have a deeper and richer understanding of what they are doing. Thus they may see God present within their experiences, and continually purify and renew their daily lives in the light of the Gospel, trying to overcome those aspects contrary to its spirit, in order to receive encouragement and support to live their lives in its light, always searching to make its truth fill their lives.

4. The celebrating community

Sunday eucharist ideally should, therefore, be the weekly 'get together' of those who are trying to continue Christ's work. We gather round the altar of the new covenant, the symbol of God's fidelity to his people; we strive for that oneness which is the sign of God's presence in the rite of reconciliation; we affirm the presence of the living Word as the scripture is proclaimed in our midst, and open ourselves to its transforming power, 'so the word that goes forth from my mouth does not return to me empty, without carrying out my will and succeeding in what it was sent to do' (Isaiah 55:11). And then we make eucharist, proclaiming the loving greatness and goodness of God in our lives and in the life of the whole world. We present ourselves to God's creative love, that God may make us holy, along with the gifts of bread and wine.

> Look with favour on your church's offering,
> and see the victim whose death has reconciled us to yourself.
> Grant that we who are nourished by his body and blood,
> may be filled with his Holy Spirit
> and become one body, one spirit in Christ.
>
> (Eucharistic Prayer III)

We enter into communion with Christ and with one another; and then, renewed and refreshed, we go forth in peace and love to take up again the gospel work of transforming society.

The Church at the Inter-face between Gospel and Non-Gospel Life and Values

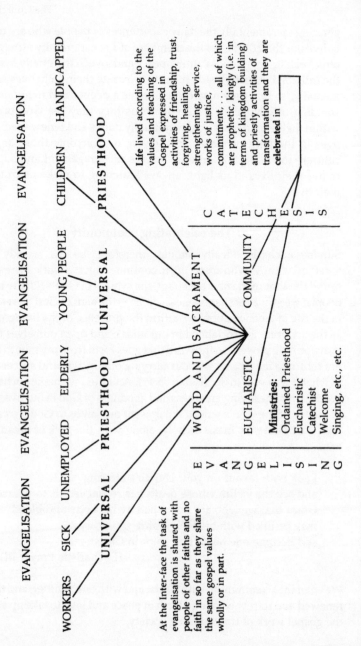

EVANGELISATION   EVANGELISATION   EVANGELISATION   EVANGELISATION   EVANGELISATION

WORKERS   SICK   UNEMPLOYED   ELDERLY   YOUNG PEOPLE   CHILDREN   HANDICAPPED

UNIVERSAL   PRIESTHOOD   UNIVERSAL   PRIESTHOOD

WORD AND SACRAMENT

EVANGELISE

EUCHARISTIC   COMMUNITY   CATECHESIS

Ministries:
Ordained Priesthood
Eucharistic
Catechist
Welcome
Singing, etc., etc.

Life lived according to the values and teaching of the Gospel expressed in activities of friendship, trust, forgiving, healing, strengthening, service, works of justice, ... all of which are prophetic, kingly (i.e. in terms of kingdom building) and priestly activities of transformation and they are **celebrated in**

At the Inter-face the task of evangelisation is shared with people of other faiths and no faith in so far as they share the same gospel values wholly or in part.

4

God: Human Experience

1. Feelings

During most of my life, as you will have gathered, God was a remote figure, someone whose existence and nature I accepted more with my mind than with my feelings: in fact, I was told not to trust my feelings about God. It took me a long time to understand and appreciate how God shared and communicated the divine to me through all my faculties including my feelings, even though I always had acknowledged that God is the author of life itself. It was my slow realisation of how God fills every aspect of life which led me to understand God's self-communication in my experience. Perhaps what actually helped me most was coming to see how Jesus spoke about God out of his own personal experience of God.

2. A feeling relationship

The image of God is central to Jesus' preaching. He described God as 'Abba', meaning 'father'. 'Abba' is the word which a small Jewish child learns to call his father from the first moment he begins to talk. Our English equivalent is 'daddy'. Now Jesus would have called Joseph 'Abba'. In other words, when Jesus wanted to tell his hearers about what God meant to him the nearest experience he had with which to compare it was his own relationship to Joseph. And so we come to know our God, who is indeed infinitely great and good, who is the First Cause, the Divine Lawgiver, as 'Abba God', as one who is entirely on our side, who is jealous for our good and happiness, whose compassion is as boundless as the sea, and takes our side against every evil which oppresses or diminishes us.

Jesus proclaimed Yahweh as 'Abba'. He did this out of his experience. He experienced this God in his life. This was not just an intellectual knowing, this was 'heart' knowledge. Jesus was wholly grasped by God. 'You are in me. I am in you' (John 17:21). And so we too are called to know this God who makes God-self known within us, and we come to know God through our experience of people and of life:

> I am Yahweh, unrivalled.
> I have not spoken in secret
> in some corner of a darkened land.
> I have not said to Jacob's descendants,
> 'Seek me in chaos'.
> I, Yahweh, speak with a directness,
> I express myself with clarity.
> (Isaiah 45:19)

And Jesus, too, endorsed the prophet. 'I bless you, Father, Lord of Heaven and of earth, for hiding these things from the learned and the clever and revealing them to mere children' (Matthew 11:25). Our God breaks into our world through our human experience.

3. Jesus: experience of life

Jesus was born into a society in which faith in God was a dominant feature of the culture. In his childhood he imbibed the faith of his parents and became versed in the religious traditions of his people. Then, as he grew into mature adulthood, he made the experienced faith of his childhood into a fully personal commitment of himself to God, and made his own the human search into the mystery of that God who was revealing God's self within creation.

What has spoken to me deeply is that theological approach which explores in depth the human life of Jesus. I suppose we are all attracted by a particular insight which we make our own, because it speaks to our experiences and we find it illuminates our understanding. What has helped me is being led to a deepening appreciation of how Jesus was totally immersed in life as we know it. He enjoyed a profound love within his own family, but felt the hatred and jealousy of those who opposed him; he admired the simple piety of many of his fellow Jews but was hurt and scandalised by the hypocrisy of some of the religious leaders; he partook of the generosity of ordinary people but was appalled by the lust for power of many in authority. And it was in and through all these experiences that Jesus struggled to make sense of his own life, find meaning for himself and discover God's presence and activity within them. As the christian story took shape in the gospels, the church took note of and underlined particular stages or facets of his journey. He was filled with joy by the Holy Spirit and blessed God for revealing hidden things to mere children (Luke 10:21-22). The gospels point to a significant moment of affirmation: 'This is my Son, the chosen one. Listen to him!' (Luke 9:36). But it was through the overwhelming experience of being deserted by this God who had affirmed him, 'My God, my God, why have you deserted me?' (Matthew 27:46) and by his clinging to that God in spite of feeling abandoned, that the church sees and proclaims the goodness and power of God revealed in resurrection, thereby giving us the grounds of our hope.

4. Searching and struggling

Jesus had no 'hot-line' to God. He was sensitive to God with a human heart and a human mind. He had to work out the implications of what it meant to be human, of what it meant to have life and have it to the full. He found himself moved by compassion at the sight of lepers, the paralysed, the blind, the outcasts and the marginalised, those against whom society erected barriers, the poor, the tax-collectors, those who did not keep the temple law. The meaning of compassion in gospel terms is to let one's innards embrace the feelings or situation of another. Jesus experienced his heart melting within him at the sight of human suffering and injustice, and in this experience understood this aspect of the human condition as belonging to death. His work of healing was his response: 'I have come so that they may have life and have it to the full' (John 10:10). His encounter with the pharisees, over what should or should not be done on the sabbath, led him to conclude that what was of its nature life-giving and a source of freedom from the dehumanising effect of slave labour had been corrupted by the touch of death, and itself had become a source of unfreedom: on the sabbath it was even forbidden to heal. His healing was life-giving, and belonged to the very essence of sabbath. Likewise, his Good News was the universality of God's loving kindness and forgiveness, which could not be boxed-in within the confines of any ritual or legal system, or reserved for a chosen few. Forgiveness was healing: healing gave life.

John's gospel emphasises that Jesus was sent by God: nevertheless Jesus had to work out each step of his mission. He felt temptation. He knew failure and frustration. Day after day he met sick and poor people trying to make sense of their lives. He clashed with people out to trick him and destroy him. Day after day these were the experiences he continually held up to the light of his own understanding of God and to the light of his own understanding of the Mosaic and prophetic tradition; and in this light he examined these experiences and happenings. In this light he looked for life; he sought out the life-giving elements of every event: these unfolded within him out of the depth of his relationship to his Father. As I write this I come to see where my own dawning understanding of John's words 'That life was the light of men' John 1:4) is leading me. Jesus had this tremendously rich grasp and appreciation of life; and it was in the light of his hold on life that he judged all that happened to him. Jesus could pick out what was lifegiving; knew instinctively where there was a touch of death. How he rejoiced at the centurion's faith: 'He was astonished', and pointed it out: 'Nowhere in Israel have I found faith like this!' (Matthew 8:10). How indignant he was with scribes and pharisees, 'You hypocrites! You who clean the outside of cup and dish and leave the inside full of extortion and intemperance' (Matthew 33:25). This led to death. Jesus preached and acted in the light of life. In every situation Jesus endorsed what was life-giving.

5. My own expenence

As I began to get in touch with experience in the life of Jesus, so I began to reflect upon experience in my own life. Up to this point I have not found it necessary to describe what I mean by experience. Perhaps I had better do so here. I distinguish passing events or happenings from experiences. At the moment all my bodily senses are reacting to various stimuli: sounds, smells, temperature, sights, etc. are all affecting me. I am comfortably seated, listening to some background music while I write. In the broadest sense of the word I am having many different experiences, or many different things are happening to me. However, I am not using the word 'experience' in this sense. I use the word to describe an event or a happening upon which I consciously reflect to make it my own and discover what meaning it has for me. Or an experience occurs when I see the implications of what is happening to me. Experience requires reflection. Insight is the fruit of reflection. Unconsciously I suppose I am always trying to make sense of everything which happens to me. Of course there can be isolated experiences in my life which I may have problems in trying to understand, but generally my past experience of life helps me to understand my day-to-day experiences of life; they form a pattern and this pattern helps me interpret new experiences which come my way; they are the tools enabling me to reflect.

I was listening to a popular song which told of the struggle a man was having in his love for a girl. The lyric was well-written; the music had a haunting quality. I was touched by it and I reflected on how difficult it was to love. The singer's struggle became my own. I realised my own pain in trying to love. It was in no sense a sweet experience, yet it was a good experience; an experience I needed to stay with because within it there was the promise of life; it was a life-giving experience.

Some years ago a man borrowed a considerable sum of money from me: he wanted it to meet some urgent needs related to a handicapped daughter. I never saw that money again, and subsequently I learnt that there was no handicapped daughter. Some months back he came to see me and told me a heart-breaking story about the same daughter. I lost my temper; I became very angry and threw him out. My anger prevented the possibility of my seeing this man as a human being; there was no way I could even begin to relate to him. The entire encounter was a bitter experience, devoid of any life-giving elements. In making it my own I discovered those elements within me which lead to death: these I could not disown, but in coming to terms with them I knew too of the paradoxical nature of the death of Christ, which offered life through forgiveness.

In both these experiences I came in touch with myself: my own difficulty in loving and my hunger for love; my outrage at being put upon and the limits of my willingness to accept others. And it was in and through these experiences that God revealed God's self to me, not as a threatening judge but as a call to a fuller life. And thus it is with all my experiences.

6. The light of life

Jesus held up his experiences to the light of his understanding of the law and the prophets seen through his experience of God as Abba. I hold up my experiences of life to the light of the life of Christ. I believe that God is forever revealing God's self through my countless experiences. This is my faith. Mark recounts Jesus saying to the people, 'Take notice of what you are hearing' (4:24); and, 'If anyone has ears to hear, let him listen to this' (4:23). This listening, this hearing is central to my faith-life; it points to an inner sensitivity to God's presence within me. I have to seek the life-enriching elements of every one of my experiences in the light of God's life within me.

There will be times when I will have to hold on to experiences of sin, frustration and failure for a long time in order for life to emerge, but because of the essential contradiction of the death of Jesus, it is here that the green shoot springs up.

5

The God who Saves us is the God who Speaks

I now feel I am moving into deep waters. What I want to present here as simply as possible are my reflections on the way God helps us to become what God wants us to be *(salvation)* and how God makes God's self known to us *(revelation)* in our world, and to do so in such a way as to remain true to the tradition; to the story of Jesus with the God-given mission of setting us free from everything which could enslave us or make us inhuman. Jesus carried out his mission through love: he loves us with a love which makes us lovable and capable of loving, a love which is the source of freedom.

1. Salvation

From the beginning, God intends everyone to reach the fullness of what God means by being human: this is salvation. God's creative and saving actions belong together.

Creation is that action of God by which God gives life and existence to the whole world. God is love. God loves the world into existence. And God loves us into existence and wants us to achieve the fullness of our being.

God loves us into existence and wants us to become fully and completely human in God's sense of what it is to be human. This is salvation. God is, therefore, everyone's God. God is both creator and saviour of every human being on the face of the earth.

Salvation, therefore, means becoming fully human. We come to know what this means through Jesus: Jesus reveals (makes known/ manifests) that the fullness of being human for which we are created involves becoming one with God as he is. This oneness with God is expressed in scripture in terms of 'sonship': Jesus is the Son of God. Each one of us is called to be 'son' or 'daughter' by adoption, made a member of God's family.

Jesus is the divine Son. Scripture speaks of the Son as being so completely one with God, that Jesus is all that God is in the created order. Jesus is God's self-expression: 'To have seen me, is to have seen the Father' (John 14:9), and God's self-realisation: 'The Father and I are one' (John 10:30).

God's plan is that we also should be God's self-expression and self-realisation. This comes about through our becoming one with Jesus: becoming 'son' or 'daughter' of God.

Now the process by which we are adopted into the family of God is the work of the Holy Spirit, the Spirit which enables us to call God 'Father'. Jesus, as the eternal Son, receives the Holy Spirit from his Father and shares this Spirit with his followers.

The Holy Spirit is the transforming Spirit, the giver of gifts (wisdom, understanding . . .), the enabler, the one who brings goodness to fruition as love, joy, peace . . . The Holy Spirit is the one who re-creates, renews, refreshes. 'I shall ask the Father and he will give you another advocate to be with you forever, the Spirit of truth' (John 14:16). 'He will teach you everything and remind you of all I have said to you' (John 14:26).

In receiving the Holy Spirit we become members of God's family, made one with Jesus. We have all clothed ourselves in Christ (Galatians 3:27) and, as Jesus was sent into the world for the world's salvation (John 3:17), so too are we sent: 'As you sent me into the world, I have sent them into the world' (John 17:18). We reach the fullness of what it is to be human (attain our salvation) in the process of helping our fellow human beings do likewise, because loving God is inseperably bound up with loving our neighbour.

Jesus spoke of saving the world, as we have already seen, in terms of establishing the kingdom of God on earth. The kingdom is a vision of life in which people live together in peace, truth, justice and love. For Jesus, as for Israel, the future of the world, and for every member of the human race, lay in God's faithfulness: 'Never again will I curse the earth because of man, because his heart contrives evil from his infancy' (Genesis 8:21). 'So now I swear concerning my anger with you and the threats I made against you. "For the mountains may depart and the hills be shaken, but my love for you will never leave you and my covenant of peace with you will never be shaken, says Yahweh who takes pity on you" ' (Isaiah 54:9-10).

As people who profess ourselves to be christian, along with a multitude of other people who share our values, we struggle to implement the vision of life which Jesus had. We live and work within God's promise never to withdraw from us the divine love. We remember our roots, we recall our story and we know that God always acts in a way that far surpasses everything we do, that God shapes the future out of the messy and muddled elements of the present. We do not know where Jesus' vision of life will take us: all we can do is to strive to make the kingdom as much a part of our present as we can.

2. Revelation

Earlier on I said that I had thought of faith as a series of great truths let down from heaven: likewise, revelation was a great package of knowledge about God brought into this world by Jesus once and for all, and handed to the Church to preserve down the centuries.

I explained that it was only after coming to understand that God is life and that God is within every aspect of life that I was able to come to terms with the idea that God is always disclosing God's self through people's experience of life.[5] Revelation, I came to see, is a process which is happening in people's lives and goes on and on. Looking back, therefore, over my own life I see how God has been at work in it, making God's self known to me through my experiences; not only through positive experiences of love, care, prayer, friendship, health, happiness but also through sin, sickness, loneliness, difficult people, failure and so on. In all the people and events of my life, God is and always has been present. Revelation is, therefore, not something which belongs simply to the past, but it is part of people's present experience of life, an experience which they can and do share with one another. This takes us back to what I said about the first witnesses to the resurrection, who shared their experiences and in so doing began the christian story.[6]

---

[5] See above, chapter 2, section 3: 'Faith and conversion', p. 37.
[6] See above, chapter 1, section 2, 'Story', p. 26.

I also said that one of the factors which helped me to a newer understanding of how God makes God's self known in life was the realisation that Jesus preached and taught out of his own experience of life, his childhood experience of the meaning of 'Abba', because his experience of God was similar to his experience of Joseph. [7]

There is however a special something about Jesus which enables us to see him revealing God in a unique way; he is the Son of God which, as we saw above, stresses and proclaims his oneness with God. And so we can say that God expresses the God's self fully and completely in Jesus, that in Jesus God realises God's self in our creation. This is what we mean when we say the Word was made flesh. God reveals God's self fully, completely and uniquely in Jesus.

In receiving the Holy Spirit, we become members of God's family. The Holy Spirit is the transforming Spirit, God's gift to us through Jesus Christ, our Lord. The Holy Spirit works in our lives to enable us to reveal God. In each of us the Holy Spirit is at work, so that we may become ways in which God continues to make God's self known in the here and now. Together we are the church in which the christian story continues in its integrity. The church, therefore, is the community of those who are struggling in faith to let the Holy Spirit transform their lives, and to become agents through whom God continues to make God's self known in our world. Further, the church works for the transformation of every single human being so that each may become son or daughter of God, and as such make God known in his/her own unique way. There is an enormous richness in the idea that every human being has something uniquely her/his own to reveal about God.

[7] See above, chapter 4, section 2, p. 51.

Part Two

Sharing Our Faith Story

6

Sharing our Faith

1. Gathering ideas together

I have been discussing God's relationship to us, and this is supremely mysterious. In the book of Exodus, Moses asks God to give him a name by which the Israelites could call upon God. God answers, 'I am who I am', which is really a polite refusal: God refuses to give him a name for God's self. In Jewish thought naming implies control: God was not going to allow God's self to be domesticated. God is sometimes spoken of as the totally other. On the one hand God is utterly different from human beings, yet on the other hand God is totally involved in creation to the extent that creation reveals, makes God known; and, in particular, we human beings make God known. The way we reveal God cannot be compared simply to the way a work of art reveals the artist, because God dwells within us in a way that no artist lives within her/his work. In fact, as we have just seen above, God is within us not simply as the source and cause of our nature and existence, but also as the one who enables us to become fully human; this means to be 'son' or 'daughter' of God.

Let me, even at the risk of being unduly repetitious, state as clearly as possible what needs to be said about revelation and communication:

● Every human being on the face of the earth discloses something of God as creator and saviour, even those who do not believe in God or whose lives contradict the divine goodness.

    — This revelation can only be 'seen' with the eyes of faith, that is by one who believes that God dwells within every member of the human race. There are many people, who have no commitment to any specific religion, who 'see' God in this way, as well as those who profess some religious commitment.

● The corollary of the above is that God discloses something of God's self within the life and being of every person on the face of the earth: 'God speaks within the human heart'; as each one struggles to deepen his/her hold on his/her experiences of life, so each one opens his/her heart to God, disclosing God's self.

— There are very many people, some of whom profess a religion and others who do not, who listen to God. Christians, because they believe in the uniqueness of Christ's revelation, will hold up these other revelations to the light of what Christ revealed, and receive them according to that light.

— We respect the way God reveals God's self in other religions, and learn from them. Our understanding of God is greatly enriched by studying different religious traditions. In our search for God we need to take into account the universal experience of humankind's search for meaning: without doing so our own searching will be impoverished.

— A very great number of people, some of whom belong to a specific religion and others who do not, have expressed personal experiences of God. These experiences of God vary from feelings about God to messages, visions, etc. They are expressions of the human heart's desire to take hold of the ultimate mystery of life. In the Christian tradition, spiritual writers offer ways of evaluating these personal experiences, based on how these experiences affirm or depart from the core-experience of the tradition as related in the christian story.

— God lives within the lives of all and discloses God's self within them, within their cultures and within their religions. Christians believe that God revealed God's self as fully as possible and in a unique way in Christ. Christ throws light on and affirms the whole human search for meaning and humankind's longing to penetrate the mystery of life, as seen in the great world religions and in the lives of individuals. In particular Christ illuminates the

Jewish tradition; and we see him as the climax of his own religious cultural tradition.

— Jesus spoke out of his own experience of God. God revealed God's self in Jesus, who communicated his understanding of God to the apostles and to the people to whom he spoke. The apostles deepened their understanding of God in the light of their experience of Jesus; and further, their experience of the risen Lord gave rise to the beginnings of the church. Within this early community the first christians reflected on their experience of Jesus, and it was out of this shared reflection that the different gospels emerged.

— The church speaks and acts out of her own experience of God. Her experience of God is one with that of Jesus' own experience of God and that of the apostles, going back to the beginning. Luke writes: 'I, in my turn, after carefully going over the whole story from the beginning have decided to write . . .' (1:3) — one continuing stream of experience down to our own day. The Holy Spirit activates and keeps alive this experience of God within the church, and makes present to her (reminds her of) past experiences of how God has ever made God's self known in the church's life. The Holy Spirit activates the church's memory in such a way that past experiences of God become an integral part of the present. Another way of explaining this would be to say that the Holy Spirit is responsible for the church's story: it is the Holy Spirit, ultimately, who is the Story Teller: she keeps alive in the hearts of the believers what has been told from the beginning.

We therefore along with other believers, who may or may not profess a religion, recognise a God who reveals God's self in and through the whole of creation and, in particular, in and through human beings, their culture and their religious traditions. Where we claim to have something special to offer is in belonging to a community which has its own story of how God reveals God's self to humankind, a story which has at its centre a unique revelation made in and communicated by Jesus Christ. Jesus himself speaks of this revelation in St John's gospel:

> If you make my word your home,
> you will indeed by my disciples,
> you will learn the truth
> and the truth will make you free.   (John 8:31-32)

'If you make my word your home' or, 'If you live within my revelation', touches upon the heart of what I am trying to say. We are members of that group of people who come together to become church and within whom God is communicating God's self in many different ways. Individual members making up the body are in touch with this God who is continually making God's self known within the lives of each of them and within them as a body. Nobody can make categoric, universal, final statements about this God. We are not just individuals but members, and it is as members that we discern God's actions and words. It is the community to which we belong which ever proclaims 'the message which was a mystery hidden for generations and centuries' (Colossians 2:26); and it is within the community that we learn the truth, the truth which makes us free.

2. Ways of sharing our faith story (1)

The church proclaims the revelation in which she makes her home through the way her members live and celebrate God-in-their-midst. In particular I draw your attention to:

a. SCRIPTURE

Scripture is the most important part of the Church's written tradition. It is the church which selected and endorsed the writings which make up the scriptures as we have them today. Their selection, and making them the chief source of guidance and inspiration for the life of the church, is part of the christian story. Scripture relates God's dealing with the human race, and has for its climax the life, death and resurrection of Jesus Christ and the beginnings of the church. Although the story is one story, it is told in a multitude of different ways, reflecting a great diversity in the way the story was seen and understood by the writers. Scripture contains, therefore, many different images of God, and hence a great diversity of theologies. Pluralism is an important facet of scripture.

b. PROPHECY

Prophecy is a dimension of the christian life which attempts to translate revelation into practical living. Being a prophet is a characteristic of being christian: prophecy belongs to the church as a whole and to individuals as members. Prophecy involves evaluating the life of groups, parties, nations, etc. and of individuals in the light of the relevation committed to the church in her living tradition, and showing how revelation can transform human life. Furthermore, integral to prophecy is the church's duty to discern God's presence and action in every aspect of humankind's life and activities, even in the lives and activities of people and nations who do not at first sight seem to accord with the church's own story.

c. LITURGY

The church makes known the revelation committed to her through the way she worships. She celebrates in word and sacrament the relationship her members have with God and with one another; and their priestly, prophetic and kingly activities of loving service in the world.

I would like here to draw your attention once more to what I said elsewhere about how one's image of God affects worship. If the community thinks of God as First Cause, Prime Mover, infinite in all perfections etc., a very stylised form of worship will tend to emerge; that is, words and actions must always be done in a certain ritualistic way. The resultant liturgy allows for no alterations. Change the image of God and immediately the form of worship is changed. What we need to remember is that we proclaim the kind of God we worship through our liturgy, the kind of God we proclaim we reflect in the way we worship.

d. WITNESS

Clearly one of the chief ways in which revelation is handed on from one generation to the next, and made known in the world, is through the way it affects the lives of Christians: they bear witness to it. Christians give this witness as they allow the teaching and values of the gospel to penetrate their thinking and attitudes, and as they make the coming of the kingdom the hope which motivates their ambitions.

e. DOCTRINE

We have the revelation. Therefore, the most obvious thing to do is simply to find different ways of articulating it and enabling the story to be handed on; but by now you will have sensed that this is a most complex issue. Here I need to spend a little time teasing this area out.

Revelation is a profoundly rich and multi-faceted concept. It can never be fully and adequately expressed, but the church throughout her history has attempted to do so in her writings. Besides the scriptures, of which I have already spoken, there are the creeds; the councils with their discussions, preambles and conclusions; works of theologians who have received universal acclaim, as well as those of others; the writings of men and women who have achieved prominence in spirituality; laws and their commentaries; the writings of popes, bishops, priests, monks, religious, laymen and women . . . the list is endless: but put it all together and you have the written form of the church's story, and this story is the story of revelation.

Now you may begin to say, 'Well, all the church has to do is to get this vast bulk of material into order, shape it and teach it'; but I am sure that even while you are saying this the crucial difficulty in handing on revelation has occurred to you. The heart of revelation is the relationship between God and the individual. The church is not handing on, ultimately, a body of knowledge but drawing human beings into a relationship with God. The question is, 'How to share a relationship?' May I remind you of the distinction between faith and beliefs: faith is the word we use of our relationship to God (I believe — I put/commit my heart in/to God); beliefs described the relationship. Faith primarily belongs to the heart, beliefs to the mind. Do you know the old saying, 'I'd rather have compunction than know its definition'?

'Well, at least, the church can make her beliefs known', you may argue and many people would agree with you, and to some extent I also agree. It is possible for the church to give a reasoned account of herself and the beliefs and traditions of which she is the guardian. St Peter thought so: 'Simply reverence the Lord Christ in your hearts, and always have your answer ready for people who ask you the reason for the hope that you all have' (1 Peter 3:13). However, I feel there is a need to qualify the giving of the 'reasoned account'. Put it this way: the heart of what the church wants to hand on is a relationship, a personal intimate loving relationship between the individual and God. Jesus expresses this relationship in his prayer to God for his friends: 'that the love with which you loved me may be in them, and that I may be in them' (John 17:26). Earlier in that same prayer, Jesus says: 'And this is eternal life, to know you, the only true God' (John 17:3). When John uses the word 'know' he means something much more than intellectual knowledge, he uses 'know' in the sense that a wife 'knows' her husband. We could perhaps use here the concept, 'heart-knowledge'. I hope I am beginning to make myself clear. We can give a reasoned account of our beliefs and traditions but no matter how much care and skill we give to producing this account it may still remain woefully inadequate, just as a wife finds it almost impossible to put into words how she loves her husband: she alone is 'in love' with him.

In this connection it is interesting to recall the practice of the early church in dealing with would-be-converts. St Ambrose, writing in the fourth century, is quite clear about this: 'Every mystery ought to be hidden and, so to speak, concealed in a faithful silence so as not to be inconsiderately published to profane ears' (De Abraham 1:38, PL 14:436). There is a very strong element of secrecy in the teaching of Jesus and, even though John relates his saying, 'I have spoken openly for all the world to hear' (John 18:20), Mark remembers, 'The secret of the kingdom of God is given to you, (the Twelve), but to those outside everything comes in parables' (Mark 4:11); and scripture uses the phrase 'uncircumcised ears', referring to those not attuned to hearing the account of things hidden.

I hope you see the kind of problems which emerge when we speak of handing on the teaching of the church; for example, how gross a simplification it is to say: 'The important thing in teaching the faith is to make sure that people (generally pupils) understand what it is all about even if they do not believe'; or 'If they don't know, they won't even know what they are rejecting.' This approach, reflected in these statements, misses the centrality of the relationship involved in sharing the faith.

3. Ways of sharing our faith story (2)

In the previous section I spoke about revelation finding its home in us, and our duty to make it known and share it with others. Here I am speaking about the teaching dimension of the church's life. The church's audience is the world, made up of peoples of all nations, of diverse cultures and races, of different religions and no religions: some ready, open and eager to listen to what we have to say if only given the opportunity; others indifferent, preferring to be left alone; again others, caught up in overt materialism or struggling to survive, simply cannot hear what we say; while still others bear a deep hostility to the church and will not listen. Such is a panoramic overview of those whom we are charged with addressing. And over and above these people, we have to deepen our own faith: we are to help each other grow in faith. Therefore re, as a result of her understanding of her task, the church has developed three main ways of sharing her story and helping people grow in faith.

a. CATECHESIS

I start with catechesis because it is the form we are probably most familiar with. Briefly, catechesis is nurture; it is the process of maturing faith. It belongs to the household of faith: it takes place among believers when they share their faith with the object of deepening and enriching it from one another's experience. It is the mutual search for meaning within the christian tradition. We acknowledge our relationship to God through and in Jesus Christ; when we are involved in catechesis we speak out of this relationship. Clearly, therefore, you cannot speak of a person who is an unbeliever being involved in catechesis; nor, it seems to me, can catechesis take place where one of the parties involved is unwilling: you cannot force catechesis upon a person.

Catechesis has the following main features:

- Catechesis takes place within the community. Christian faith should always have a community dimension and it should lead to a deepening of community. I am not saying that in catechesis one is looking to the community for all the answers to life's mysteries: the community itself is a learning community.

- Catechesis helps us to develop our gospel vision of life: this means deepening our understanding of how our faith works itself out in the practical details of everyday living. The gospel sets out for us a vision of life; it offers us a hierarchy of values; it prompts us to change our attitudes; educates us by helping us to understand the meaning of true liberty; and it guides and leads us to commit ourselves to the task of changing society from a 'kingdom' perspective, and to the task of working for the integral development of humanity. At its heart is the mysterious dialogue between God and humanity.

— Catechesis is a sharing of beliefs, values, ideas. It is a mutual learning process. This sharing will, as the occasion demands (in the case of would-be-converts and children, for example) include a systematic programme to cover every aspect of the christian's relationship to God, the church and humankind so that everybody may have a thorough grounding for their faith-life.

— Catechesis involves prayer: not only instruction on individual prayer but also on the communal prayer-life of the church: for example, the eucharist.

— Catechesis is a life-long process. There is never a point at which catechesis is completed, because there is no point in human life at which the individual can encompass God.

Before continuing, I want to make two points:

i. I would like to add that while I have detailed the main features of catechesis it does not follow that all the elements described will necessarily always be present in every example of catechesis. And, moreover, certain features of catechesis are more appropriate at certain times than at others. For example in the case of the catechesis of adolescents it is appropriate to put considerable emphasis on the practical living out of their faith commitment by encouraging them to become involved in some form of service. The catechesis will then develop out of their reflections on what they are doing. Catechesis always demands reflection.

ii. I want to emphasise that catechesis is educational: it is part of the whole process of education through which individuals are helped to grow up and develop their full potential as human beings. It calls upon students to make full use of their intellectual skills and abilities, to evaluate and assess critically the content of catechesis: yet at the same time one has to remember that, as with all personal relationships and commitment, there will always remain a place for wonder, to which reason can only point the way.

b. EVANGELISATION

In the first place evangelisation describes our approach to those who do not belong to the household of the faith. It involves taking the good news to those who have little or no sense of the divine dimension of life and whose lives are rooted in materialism and who have a distorted understanding of what it means to be human. Evangelisation attempts to transform people from within themselves through the divine power of the message which it proclaims. It urges them to interpret their experiences in the light of the gospel. It challenges them with the vision of the kingdom and the new way of living implied by it. It appeals not only to individual consciences but also to the collective conscience of people; it strives to influence the activities in which people are engaged and the concrete environment of their lives. As they become aware of Christ they find themselves being challenged by his values and teaching and the implications which result for their life style.

In the second place, evangelisation has also a place in the lives of believers, that is, among ourselves who form the household of faith. Conversion is a life-time process; we spend the whole of our lives struggling to be freed from the cloying effects of paganism by the power of the gospel; we need to undergo conversion after conversion in order to deepen our commitment to Christ and to his values and way of living. Sometimes this form of evangelisation, because it deals with the believer, is called *evangelising catechesis*. And, because it involves both conversion and the deepening of faith it is *the most frequently used form* of sharing our faith.

N.B. I feel a need here to emphasise that the Church wants people to repent, to change and believe the Good News. She makes every effort to help people come to know God's loving kindness and to have an opportunity to learn about Christ. She does her best to create the conditions which lead to conversion. However conversion is conversion to a loving relationship with God which involves people giving themselves freely to God. Hence anything which violates this freedom or mars human dignity is completely abhorrent to her.

c. RELIGIOUS EDUCATION

It is precisely because of the dignity and freedom of the individual that the whole concept of religious education has evolved. The very nature of education involves the freedom and dignity of the pupil: its concern is how to help pupils develop their full potential as human beings. This dignity and freedom is threatened where the pupils are told by an authority (which they are taught to accept and respect by the cultural context of their lives) what to believe. Education, to be true to its nature, cannot tell people what to believe: all it can do is to say what people do believe. Teachers can help pupils understand what catholics believe: they cannot make them believe it. Hence the classroom is not the right setting for deliberately evangelising pupils nor is it the place where catechesis normally occurs.

At the outset I think it is important to see that religious education belongs to the sphere of education; therefore, whatever takes place under this umbrella must satisfy the norms of education. I think it would only make this section extremely ponderous if I embarked on a lengthy discussion of the nature of education. So it will have to suffice to say I believe that education is not ultimately about learning facts and figures nor about how to do this or that more effectively, but is concerned with the development of the whole person as a thinking, feeling, relating, doing human being. Education is the art of facilitating the process of becoming fully human. It is not the handing on of ready-made beliefs, ideas, images, values etc. but the learning to see, to listen, to discern, to feel, to imagine, to hope, to love, to choose, to wish, to believe . . . and to make sense of oneself and the world.

Education is very much concerned with meaning — that is with helping people make sense of themselves and of the world in which they live. Religious education is, therefore, about 'meaning' and the need to discover answers for oneself to the basic questions about human existence: where I do I come from?; where am I going?: who am I?: why pain, suffering, death? Is there a future . . .? Religious education does not give categoric answers to these questions; it helps people to see that being human means to be concerned with these questions and to search for answers which will help one to make sense of one's life. It is concerned with that area of human life which we call spiritual.

One of the ways in which it operates is to examine the ways different people do search for meaning and the kind of answers they come up with: so, for example, it strives to convey what it means to be a Muslim and how Muslims discover meaning for their lives. It does this by helping to equip the student with the skills of dealing with religious concepts (the skills of informed criticism, rational judgement, and the consequent capacity to think for oneself) and how to use these skills to enter into the ideas, feelings, attitudes, beliefs, values, activities, ways of worship, etc. of a Muslim: and similarly of those of other faiths and no faith (what does it mean to be an atheist?). Thus religious education leads students to have a sympathetic understanding of religion without attempting to impose or influence their position: nevertheless, it may well challenge the stance adopted by some students.

Such an education leads to mature freedom and constructs a platform, as it were, on which individuals can stand to make a faith-commitment or a thoughtful rejection; but, whether they make a commitment or not, they learn to have true empathy with and to savour the religious realm of the meaning of life; and they learn to value it in the process of their own development as human beings, and in their search for the meaning of life.

I need to add a final observation. I have been presupposing that in a school setting (this may apply to a Sunday parochial congregation) the pupils range over a whole spectrum of commitment: some will come from very committed christian catholic families and some may be themselves committed; others, the exact opposite. When, therefore, religious education is presented to pupils of such wide-ranging commitment, it will be received in different ways: some will receive it as 'catechesis', some may well be evangelised by it, while others will hear it simply as religious education.

Religious education does not belong simply to the classroom, though I have been discussing it from that perspective. It is a life-long process. We need continually to be helped to understand religion and its importance in our lives.

Earlier in this section I said that the classroom was not an appropriate setting in which to evangelise pupils deliberately. I am not saying that the gospel has no place in classrooms — far from it: one hopes that the gospel pervades all that takes place in those rooms both with regard to the teachers' values and life-style and the attitudes they have towards society, their relations to the pupils and the pupils' relations among themselves.

With regard to catechesis in the classroom, historically, the school was part of the christian community and parents extended their duty of giving their children a christian upbringing to the teachers: the phrase *'loco parentis'* means precisely this. In such a setting, where all the pupils came from committed christian homes and the parents wanted their children to be given an education in the faith, catechesis may well have taken place in the classroom: there could have been a genuine faith-sharing, though even in these circumstances the question of freedom arises. However, these circumstances are being found less and less often in our schools; more and more parents remain uncommitted; many of them send their children to catholic schools for non-religious reasons.

Furthermore, I am not at all sure that the dispositions expressed in the situation in which uncommitted parents send their children to a catholic school, in order to be taught their religion, are sufficient for catechesis: I believe the truth of the old adage that in matters of faith the school can only complement the home; it cannot take its place and give the child what the home does not. The situation has, therefore, radically changed and, with a significant number of pupils in every class, faith-sharing is no longer possible. Now, if it is inappropriate for some, can it be given to the others? I think not (that is, not in the same classroom with the others). For the reasons, I refer you back to my reflections on 'profane ears', and to those on evangelisation and the danger of proselytism.[8] Therefore I believe catechesis may well not be appropriate to a class-room setting. May I add, however, that a place should be found for it within a school in a situation where pupils freely choose to attend; for example, catechesis may happen in a Justice and Peace group reflecting on how they should respond to a particular issue. I think catechesis can occur among very young children and their teacher. Later we shall see that young children have a unique religious dimension in their lives, as one observes in their sensitivity to mystery and their readiness to wonder; and it is out of this religious dimension that they do catechesis. The older the children become the less appropriate is catechesis as the direct aim of the teacher for all the children in the classroom, although as I have suggested above, some children will receive what they are being taught as catechesis.

[8] See above, pp. 68f.

7

Stages of the Journey

1. Growing faith

An enormous amount of work has been done during this century on how individuals develop, physically, psychologically, religiously, intellectually, morally. Obviously I am very concerned with this subject. However, I can neither make an adequate presentation of all that has been written, even on what is most pertinent, namely, religious development; nor can I give a critical evaluation of the thinking on this subject. All I can do here is to present some ideas which make sense to me about how a child develops religiously through childhood into adolescence, which I hope will throw light on what is happening in the formation of our children today. I say 'throw light', not 'solve'.

I have made much of faith as a journey because I find this a helpful metaphor, and because it is a very traditional image. What it says to me is that our faith is something which grows and develops until, through our death and resurrection, faith gives way to vision. I believe that everybody makes this journey at his/her own pace: there is no way to programme people's faith-journey, as ultimately progress is reckoned in terms of how each one responds to God's inviting grace; and perhaps the most important thing about the journeying is the struggling to respond to that grace. Finally, I think it is important for individuals to believe that it is all right for them to be where they are on the journey, and not to feel guilty because they do not seem to be where others are.

I am, therefore, considering faith as a journey involving inner growth and an ever-deepening awareness, and I believe that what moves us along the journey is God's love drawing us to God's self. The question arises, can we plot this journey? Can we describe particular stages of it? This is precisely the question which experts on faith development attempt to answer.[9]

Here I would like to make a few preliminary observations. Faith, as we have seen, enables us to make sense of life. The way small children make sense of their world is clearly different from the way adolescents do; and so faith, in this sense, changes and develops as people attempt to cope with the world as they encounter it at the different points in their lives. Faith changes and develops when individuals are challenged by an event or a crisis in their lives which questions their presently held belief system: death, pain and anxiety question an image of God which does not allow for personal suffering. Similarly, faith can change when we meet another whose faith-outlook makes us examine our own and makes us wonder what it is that drives the other to be the person she/he is. The obvious example here is the individual's encounter with Christ and being challenged by his faith. Similarly, faith can change through being with one's fellow believers, worshipping and working together. Faith may grow deeper through prayer and through being challenged by the gospel.

2. Beginning to journey

Love is the setting in which most children emerge into the world. It is within this love that children begin their faith-journey. Meaning, we have seen, is not the same as faith: to have grasped the meaning of different aspects of life is not the same as to have faith. Nevertheless, faith is intimately connected with meaning: it is through my faith that I make sense of my life and find meaning in the world. Infants cope with themselves and the bleak world into which they have been ushered through the love, care and security with which they are enfolded: this makes sense for them. In responding to this felt love, they are responding to the creative and salvific presence of God deep within life itself.

A relationship implies a mutual self-giving: mothers and fathers give themselves knowingly and willingly to their babies, desiring to love them into existence. At some point, perhaps almost immediately, there is a response to this love in their children, discernible perhaps

[9] See Bibliography.

only to the parents; but it is deep within the beginning of this relationship that the faith-journey begins, not just for children from a family which has an avowed religious commitment, but for every child; not just for those whose parents can name God's presence and action in their babies' lives, but for every baby.

The writer, John Westerhoff, examining the faith-journey distinguishes what he calls four different 'styles of faith'.[10] The first of these he calls 'experienced faith': the children experience the faith of their parents and of other significant adults in their lives. Children imbibe their attitudes and values, and begin to accept their way of looking at the very many experiences which impinge upon them as they explore and examine themselves and their environment. But these small children are not simply empty vessels into which information is poured; nor, to change the metaphor, just supple and pliable beings who can be shaped by the whim of the adult world. They have a profound religious sense, and they are readily in touch with a whole dimension of unending mystery and unalloyed wonder. Wonder and awe at everything about them come quite naturally to children. The world is a mystery. What we articulate as the 'divine' is everywhere manifest for them in life's daily miracles. Ultimate questions about life and death, the purpose and nature of the universe, arise quite naturally. This rich experience of wonder and mystery gives birth to the child's first essay at coming to terms with the world. God and the gods people the world, along with dragons and fairies: these fantasy figures weave in and out of children's experiences; they become involved through their imagination in the never-ending struggle between the forces of good and evil, which at times impinge upon them with great intensity as deep happiness; at other times, as real fear. It is precisely here that the story is so powerful and important, for it creates a secure world by assuring children of the ultimate triumph of the good prince over the evil dragon. The security of being loved and the assurance of the ultimate triumph of good are the basic religious experiences upon which human life is built, and from within which the faith-journey proceeds and life is found to be meaningful. Out of our own under-

---

[10] *Will our Children have Faith?* (see Bibliography). Westerhoff names the styles of faith: experienced, affiliative, searching and owning. No sooner does one begin to 'own' than one begins again to 'search'.

standing of creation and salvation, we believe that this love and this meaningful security are the 'given' of human existence — every single individual's human birthright. Without these religious experiences, no boundaries exist and the individual is exposed to the chaos of meaninglessness.

The function of the fairy story, therefore, is to help children to feel secure in the world: it assures them that wickedness is finally defeated, beauty overcomes ugliness and happiness finally banishes sorrow. The modern fairy story places the cosmic struggle between good and evil in space, with characters proficient in modern technology, and although many of these tales carry with them a certain ambiguity there remains an ultimate hope in the survival of humankind. The anti-hero may figure in modern culture, but she/he only throws into relief the human desire for a victor with whom people can identify. Deep down in the human heart there is not only a hope but also a belief in a 'happy ending'.

Perhaps what I am emphasising is simply our profound belief in ourselves: that in spite of the most horrendous self-inflicted disasters there persists an almost incredible belief in the greatness and dignity of being human. We catch glimpses of this in how the Jews lived through and survived the Nazi attempt to obliterate their race in the Holocaust: they proclaimed how human beings triumph over the most sadistic and evil humiliations. It is this belief which finds expression in the *Universal Declaration of Rights* approved by the General Assembly of the United Nations in 1948, when nations of every creed and no creed asserted: 'All human beings are born free and equal in dignity and rights.'

This belief is about the survival of the human race, which one generation inherits from its predecessor and passes on to the next. It is this belief which parents fumble, incoherently at times, to pass on to their children in their instinctive desire to do their 'best' for their offspring. Some indeed may have a very jaundiced view of humankind and may not profess a belief that the ultimate ground of humankind is good; nevertheless, they organize their children's world so that their children may feel safe and secure. This belief stands at the beginning of the faith-journey. Christian parents will speak about it in the light of the christian story; parents of other religions will speak out of their tradition: parents of no religious convictions will, nevertheless, not be lacking in providing suitable myths to secure the world for their children.

The christian story affirms what I have been striving to put into words. We noted earlier how Jesus proclaimed, out of his own personal experience of the world, that in spite of its contradictions and ambiguities he believed that the ultimate ground of its being was a God whom he could only describe as 'Abba': a caring and loving God who would, in and through creation, ultimately triumph over the powers of darkness. This adult, mature faith of Jesus had been shaped in his childhood by the faith of his parents, whose own understanding of the world was rooted in Israel's story of how Yahweh God had chosen them as a people in whom Yahweh could make God's self known as a loving and caring God. It was in the light of this faith that Joseph and Mary helped Jesus interpret his childhood experiences and overcome his fears. The good prince (David) slew the wicked dragon (Goliath)! Good defeats evil: so Mary and Joseph created a secure environment in which their child could grow and mature. Not only did Mary and Joseph do this, but they helped Jesus discover within himself resources to cope with what frightened him. Similarly, all parents build up their children's confidence in themselves. Christian believers will speak of trusting in God, who cares for them: but whether parents believe in God or not, the ability to cope with life's problems and fears is the gift of God.

3. First steps

Therefore, the beginnings of the journey rest on:

- creating a secure world in which the child can live

- achieving this by assuring the child of the ultimate triumph of good over evil

- using stories as a methodology to bring this about

- leading the children to believe that they have within themselves the inner resources to cope with the world

Everything that God stands for in these beginnings is so identified with her/his parents that the child does not make any distinction, nor need she/he. In the first years every individual has a profound faith, though unformulated, and one we underestimate at our peril in an evolving religious formation.

The next step in the faith-journey also uses story as its methodology, as children begin to learn what the family of which they are now part thinks and believes. 'We do things this way. We've always done them so. These are the things we believe!' Children pick up the ways and beliefs of the family, and desperately want to do so, because they want to feel that they belong to and are accepted by the adult world of their immediate environment. Now there are not only 'fairy' tales, but stories about the family and about individual members, stories about the place where they were born and in which they all live, stories about shops and streets, stories about other people, stories . . . As the child grows older so the variety of the stories grows: legends (including specifically religious stories) form a bridge to real heroes and heroines,[11] and enrich the basic religious truths. Slowly children accept the ways and attitudes of their parents,[12] who support them as they continue to try to make sense of their world and find security.

Gabriel Moran describes this stage as acquiring 'Our own People's Beliefs': the child learns how to get along in life; including, where it is relevant, how the family worship. The kind of faith belonging to this phase is called by John Westerhoff 'affiliative'.

The more I reflect upon this stage in a child's religious development, the more certain I am that we frequently misinterpret what is going on. At this time children are expressing chiefly their great desire to belong and to be a real part of their world; this can result in their attempts to please parents and teachers by being religious; they can appear very righteous and show many of the characteristics of a much more mature faith. This happens especially around the time of their first communion. This can be a time for some children to imagine themselves as priests and nuns. The important thing is to recognize what is happening, encourage the goodness in their efforts but carefully deflect its excesses; as, for example, by not interpreting what is going on in terms of priestly or religious vocations.

In the year (perhaps two years) following first sacraments, Westerhoff's 'affiliative' faith continues to be the child's style of faith. But

---

[11] Gabriel Moran, *Religious Educatioin Development*, (Winston Press, 1983).
[12] John Westerhoff, *Will our Children have Faith?*

then an uneasiness begins to emerge, and is well established before the children's frustration with the confines of the primary school and their desire for a wider horizon really make themselves felt. However, because of the close world of the primary school community, children have difficulty in getting in touch with this uneasiness and have even more difficulty in expressing it.

The last thing we should be surprised about is that frustration and uneasiness exist: transition there must be. Once we may have placed this transition wholly within the secondary school, but not any more. We have to take into account not only the earlier age at which children are physically maturing but the diversity and multiplicity of experiences characteristic of society today. The pressing problem of television is not its sorties into sex and violence (alarming though these may be) but its materialism, which challenges a faith which proclaims that the ultimate triumph of good over evil is not wholly within the power of human beings, and that a human being's inner resources depend on a power which transcends the 'human'. Exposure to the intricate skills of the computer and that of the doctor replacing defective parts of the human body, and the triumphs of machines in space, no matter how good these achievements are in themselves, can only lead the child to question the existence of an unseen power not subject to human scrutiny and control: 'All day long men say to me, "Where is your God?" ' (Psalm 42).

It seems to me, therefore, that some time in the years after first holy communion, we enter another phase of religious development — a period of transition. The transition is very gradual: at its beginning, to all appearances, very little of significance may appear to be different. The children are, in fact, coping satisfactorily with the clash between received religious truth and a world of expanding horizons, which does not fit snugly into this pattern of religious thinking, by relying on the authority of adults (parents and teachers) who still govern their lives very strongly. I think it is important to underline the phrase 'children succeed in coping . . .' They do have something to cope with! Clearly, the extent to which they have to cope at this time depends on how protective their immediate family circle is and how exposed they are to secular influences, but sooner or later these influences are going to make an impact on their lives greater than the authority which presently sustains them.

There is, therefore, a need in the years following the reception of first holy communion to be somewhat 'laid back' (if one might use that rather appropriate americanism) with regard to the presentation of religion in the classroom. Religious education is the classroom subject. Teachers need to create situations in which aspects of the clash between the reality of religious truth and materialism can emerge, and can be dealt with in a relaxed and sympathetic way. Children know by the very way mathematics, history, science are presented that they are but at the beginnings of these subjects and that there remain to be explored vast areas which will occupy them for the rest of their years of schooling. They must have the same feeling with regard to religion. We have to combat the desire to give them the whole package immediately. Somehow or other we need to convey the ideas of 'searching' and 'journeying'.

4. Journeying and searching

I am avoiding being too categoric with regard to the actual age of the child when these different stages of faith development take place. Experienced faith of infancy and early childhood gives way to affiliative faith (acquiring our own people's beliefs) and somewhere, a year or two before the end of primary school, the transition towards another stage begins. The transition takes place because the children's faith stance,[13] the way they make sense of the world, cannot cope with the vast amount of information, nor with the multiplicity of experiences, flooding into their lives. Although the actual transition begins before the end of primary schooling, its surfacing and verbal expression only begin when the children move into secondary schooling: and it happens at this time because the kind of authority which governs childhood gives way to a new kind of authoritative framework involving greater individual freedom and responsibility; and, moreover, it is at this time that the power of the peer group becomes a felt factor in their lives in a completely new way. Add to all this their awakened sexual powers, and pupils begin to feel sufficiently free as they settle down to secondary schooling to question the beliefs, practices and

---

[13] It may be happening among girls before boys, but be contained by a greater degree of conformism among the former than the latter.

values they have so far acquired. John Westerhoff calls this style of believing, 'searching faith'. I think it is necessary to point out, in order to put it into its proper perspective, that this searching is but one activity in a whole multiplicity of happenings which occupy the attention of adolescents at this time.

a. THE EXUBERANCE OF ADOLESCENCE

Adults find adolescents the most difficult of all people to deal with, but for children entering adolescence it is like entering a new world full of new possibilities and challenges. They experience occasions of great personal fulfilment, while at other times they experience frustration and failure; they feel the pull of the future and what they can become, while hankering for the securities of their passing childhood. Adolescence must not be thought of simply as a period to be endured or as a corridor to adulthood, but as a time to be enjoyed and made the most of. Adolescents must be given freedom to experiment, to hold outrageous opinions and to try different styles of living; to break their hearts while at the same time being offered a secure framework within which to do all these things.

All this must be borne in mind as I come to speak in greater detail of this stage in the faith-journey. We have to approach the searching of adolescence with great wisdom by treating adolescents with great sensitivity on the one hand, yet not being over-serious with them on the other hand.

b. DISBELIEF

As they make their way through secondary school, the very clarity and completeness of an earlier presentation of religion backfires. Good teachers will have tried to present their pupils with a system of beliefs and a coherent picture of the universe in a biblical and doctrinal setting. Now, as pupils develop new thinking skills and begin to be at home with abstractions, they are able to take their first steps in critical evaluation and, as it were, are now ready to sharpen these critical claws on religion. Does the system of beliefs and the authoritative picture of the universe which they were taught stand up to the cool appraisal of critical judgement? They ask questions which seek to test and validate what they have been told: they want proof. To adults they can sound impudent and defiant. This is the age of disbelief! I am using disbelief and distinguishing it from unbelief, a distinction I have taken from Gabriel Moran. By unbelief Moran means a well-thought-out position: disbelief is more of an immediate reaction as, for example, 'A look of total disbelief crossed his face when I said God loved him and would do anything for him.' Children entering this new stage of their faith-journey begin to disbelieve the beliefs that they have acquired; because they, like other elements of childhood, belong to a stage which is becoming past history and which appears to them as too limiting for the next leg of the journey towards adulthood. Frequently, the stronger their religious upbringing, the stronger the reaction will be. Such is human perversity!

Parents, teachers and other significant adults, when faced with this phase of 'disbelief', must not over-react. Adolescents are quite likely to espouse confrontation, simply to test their elders' belief system and how seriously their 'betters' accept it. They enjoy being outrageous and they need someone to kick against. It is precisely at this particular point that school chaplains, house masters/mistresses, sponsors can be most helpful. Everybody concerned needs to remember that 'disbelief' makes the next step possible; that is, finding the answer to: 'What do I really believe?'

c. TRAVELLING IN ORDER TO BELIEVE

During the years of secondary schooling children need to be supported by parents and other adults who are important to them: they need to see how the religious education which they are receiving works itself out in real life. Above all, they must be helped to appreciate the need to believe and the value of believing. At the moment I am not talking about *'what'* to believe but about that activity called *'believing'*; it is intimately connected with having a purpose in life and making sense of our lives and the world in which we live. 'To be human is to live in a world composed not of things, but of meanings. To be deprived of meaning is to be without understanding, and to be without understanding is to be, not a human being, but a stranger to the human condition.'[14] When I speak of understanding, I am talking

---

[14] M. Oakeshott, Paper to the Philosophy of Education Society of Great Britain, January 1970: 'Education: The Frustration and the Engagement' in an anthology put together by Bearden, Peters and Hurst. I came across a reference to Oakeshott in an incomplete but excellent paper I have in my possession: 'The Education of a Christian Teacher'; it is incomplete in that there are no notes and its author is not named.

about something more than just a rational process; it involves an appreciation of life belonging to the whole person. Mentally-handicapped persons are certainly not without an understanding of life, even though they may not be able to articulate it. Good education, religious and secular, is not acquiring a stock of ready-made systems of ideas, images, sentiments, beliefs, etc. It is learning to look, to listen, to think, to feel, to imagine, to have faith, to understand, to choose, and to wish and, may I add, to love and to dream.[15]

Religious education is learning about the importance of believing, of holding certain beliefs and of living according to the values which result: this learning is an essential part of the process of becoming human. Human beings need to make sense of themselves and the world in which they live. If I am presented simply with *what* to believe during these my most impressionable years (a system of beliefs and values as the *one* and *only truth* and *explanation* of myself and the world) and I reject this truth and explanation, there is a danger that I will drift into meaninglessness. There is no alternative! However, if I am also taught about believing and the search for meaning and how other people believe and find values, thus making sense of their lives, then if I reject what I first received at least I will feel the need to continue to search!

d. VALUES

I think you will agree, parents and teachers, that adolescent disbelief is directed more at the package of beliefs and practices, going to Mass, confession, etc. than at the values which flow from them. As much as anything else, adolescents reject the way the belief system is articulated, and the credibility gap between the articulation and how it is lived out in practice. As a result they question and challenge in ways which on the surface imply outright rejection. Nevertheless, throughout this period when youngsters try their wits against religious beliefs, basic religious values of love and care, loyalty and courage continue to influence them. Many indeed will commit themselves to the whole field of justice, and work out their personal uncertainties in righteous indignation. One of the areas of their value system, however, in which there is considerable 'disbelief', is that which touches

[15] Ibid.

upon sexual morality, as might well be expected, because here they are subject to powerful forces which bring with them their own ambiguity and confusion. Yet even here, a strange paradox may emerge that, while rejecting much of the church's teaching, they construct a rigid morality for themselves.

e. GOOD SELF-IMAGE

A few paragraphs back I was talking about disbelief as defined by Gabriel Moran. I think the reason why 'disbelief' takes some time to show itself is that these young teenagers are so busy with so many other aspects of growing up that they are not interested in putting their beliefs into words and do not have the time to tackle what some people call the religious problem. They simply let it ride. Primarily, they are concerned with their own identity, in answering the question: 'Who am I?', and this is inextricably tied into their developing sexuality. There is probably no one single issue more important for these youngsters than to be able to come to terms with themselves and acquire a proper self-respect: a good self-image! It is only out of a sense of one's own value that personal relationships can be established and deepened, and one is able to live with the more ambiguous aspects of one's character. We ourselves have to remember continuously that the heart of friendship is the gift of ourself to the other: we must value what we give. Similarly, the only way I can cope with the dark side of myself, in spite of being a sinner, is knowing that I am loved and valued for myself and not for what I do. Coming to terms with self-identity takes place in the midst of a multiplicity of activities. Secondary schooling with its new freedoms, making a place for oneself amid one's peers, sensing and testing new parental attitudes, form the background to the pursuits and interests of adolescence. Sport, music, money, clothes, hobbies, computers, videos — the whole consumer package — along with the urge to be successful, do not leave much time for these young people to be over-involved in official institutional religion. They find themselves fully occupied trying to make sense of all their new experiences and discovering an answer to 'Who am I?'

f. TODAY'S CHALLENGE

Because adolescents tend to shy away from official religion, it does not make what is happening in their lives any less religious. The search to make sense of the multiplicity of experiences taking place within them is a religious search. Today's world, containing as it does the threat of nuclear annihilation, questions their childhood belief that good triumphs over evil. In their own immediate society the possibility of unemployment undermines the theoretical basis of their schooling: that hard work is the key to success; and that other childhood belief, that they have within themselves the inner resources to cope with life's dark forces. I believe that where there is a clash between this age-group and the adult world the cause of it may possibly be found in adolescents feeling that they have been cheated: 'You made us believe in the ultimate triumph of good over evil. The evidence is against you!' Putting it this way may seem surprising, but the point is that it requires a more mature faith than that which is common among adolescents to cope with the underlying tensions of good and evil.

8

Process

1. There are all sorts of service

I want to begin this section by quoting St Paul:

> There is a variety of gifts but always the same spirit: there are
> all sorts of service to be done, but always to the same Lord;
> working in all sorts of different ways in different people, it is
> the same God who is working in all of them. The particular
> way in which the Spirit is given to each person is for a good
> purpose (1 Corinthians 12:4 ff).

Paul then goes on to detail 'preaching with wisdom', 'preaching
instruction', 'the gift of faith', 'the gift of recognizing spirits', 'the gift
of tongues', 'the abililty to interpret them'. Different gifts to different
people but to each person the spirit is given. The people of God is a
gifted people!

Perhaps Paul is doing no more than reminding his audience, the
Corinthians, of the basic truth that all that they have, all that makes
them the kind of people they are, is God's gift. There was no doubt
every reason for Paul to remind his readers of this truth, as there is
every reason for us to remember how we have been gifted. It seems to
me that it is out of this understanding of being gifted by God that 'ministry', in the church's understanding of that word, emerges. We have
been given the responsibility of proclaiming the gospel and sharing
our faith by our baptism. If we are to be true to our calling and to the
presence of the Holy Spirit within our lives as christians, we cannot
but offer to others what we have received, in season and out of season:
this responsibility must continually affect every aspect of our rela-

tionships with other people. Therefore, ministry in this broadest sense is using our native wit, graced by the Holy Spirit, to share our faith with other people. Thus husbands and wives exercise a ministry to each other, parents to their children, teachers to their pupils, friends to each other, christians to strangers. We christians all minister to one another, to those of other faiths, and to those of whom Christ speaks as being in the dark.

However, when we hear our christian story, we are reminded that from the very beginning our people believed it important to clarify the various kinds of ministries which had to be performed and to detail definite individuals to fulfil them.[16] Our forbears were already involved in preaching and teaching (evangelising and catechising), praying together, celebrating eucharist (breaking bread together), curing and comforting the sick, caring for the poor, when they realized that the life of the community needed more structure and more organization. As an immediate result, deacons emerged and were officially delegated to take charge of 'good works'; the widows would no longer have cause to complain (Acts 6:1 ff)! And so slowly within our community it became customary for certain people to be designated and delegated to fulfil specific areas of the community's apostolic thrust. Therefore, we began to have individuals whose special concern it was to offer hospitality, to care for the sick, to pray, to travel and evangelise, to look after the old, to give alms, to sing, to catechise, to preside at eucharist, to be managing director or overseer. However, out of a long historical evolution the ministries of bishop and priest eventually came to predominate and, I suppose, from our own experience of the church, it is these which stand out and which we think are the only ones which matter. Nevertheless, when we look at our church community today, world-wide and in our own country, we find the laity beginning to assume responsibilities which previously had been held only by the ordained ministry. These will vary from running the parochial accounts to organising the Sunday liturgy.

Here I would like to pause and look at the growth and the development of a child's faith in the light of ministry. The nurture of a child's faith is the responsibility of the local parish community, though the

---

[16] What is said here about ministries is further developed below, chapter 12, section 4, 'Transforming vision', p. 136.

immediate ministers of the child's faith are the parents and other significant adults in the child's life. The responsibility of the parish begins at baptism and continues throughout the baptised person's life, though it may be exercised in very many different ways and degrees of intensity.

Logically, the next ministers are the children's schoolteachers, both as individuals and collectively. I put it this way because as individuals they are responsible for what goes on in the classroom: collectively, along with the school governors and the local clergy, for the gospel atmosphere of the school. Over the years teachers are in a position to play a very important ministry during childhood and adolescence, in the sphere of life itself and in the academic and religious spheres: in fact, they have the unique task of marrying these spheres together. The role of teachers needs to be understood on the background of what I have said previously about evangelisation, catechesis and religious education.[17]

In recent years the preparation for first confession and holy communion and for confirmation has been done more and more in the parish. In this situation parents have been invited to become involved in the actual preparation of their children by catechists. Thus, the very ancient ministry of the catechist has once more appeared in the church. True, some teachers have always acted as catechists, but here I am speaking of the catechist as a recognized ministry. Catechists are beginning to play an important role, not just in the lives of children, but in the life of the parish as a whole. We need to explore in people's lives opportunities when an ever deepening catechesis can be offered. There is a relevant catechesis for the whole of life, for every stage of growth and development.

We have therefore parents, friends, teachers and catechists, in fact the whole community, playing an immediate and active part in the children's faith-journey. In that community the priests too have a special place: what they do through formal and informal liturgies, especially the eucharist, and their involvement in the children's first reception of confession and holy communion, and later with regard to confirmation, is of immense significance: it can lay the foundations of very enriching future relationships.

---

[17] See above, chapter 6, section 3, pp. 69ff.

This then is the network we set up to support our children on their faith-journey. In a way everybody so far mentioned has a fairly clearly-defined task, but there is another role which is less easily definable and yet is equally, if not more, important: that is the role of confidant. Children in their faith-journey need someone with whom they can talk over what is happening in their lives, with whom they can share their doubts and problems and from whom they can receive assurance. In formal spirituality this is the function of the spiritual director. In the lives of children it could be their parents or teachers or catechists or priests who fulfil this role. Historically, this role was fulfilled by godparents or sponsors. All I want to do here is to draw your attention to it: children need the equivalent of a spiritual director. They need someone at a personal, individual level to listen to them and to help them get in touch with their experiences and understand them, and further to help them make the religious teaching they receive their own. They want also to hear how other people try to lead a christian life.

2. How we serve

How do we accompany people on their faith-journey? How do we help people grow in faith?

At the beginning of this section I want to place the following quotation from an unknown hand:

> Our first task in approaching another people, another culture, another religion, is to take off our shoes, for the place we are approaching is holy;
> else we might find ourselves treading on another's dream.
> More serious still, we may forget that God was there before us.

Another people, another culture, another religion and another person! Before we begin to share our faith with anyone we must remember that God has gone before us. God is already present within the lives of the people whom we wish to serve, not simply as their creator, but also as their saviour. God is present, drawing them to God's self. The next thing we have to remember is that when we speak of salvation we are talking about reaching the fullness of what it means to be human as

God has designed us to be human. We are trying to help people reach their full potential as human beings; therefore, our task is to encourage and aid all that is really human in them. Our model for what it is to be human is made known to us in Jesus.

What exactly are we doing when we share our faith with others? We are offering others what we believe from out of a whole pool of beliefs, values and symbols which describe our relationship to God, to other people and to the world. Our creed, code and cult have been handed down to us from the past: they are part of the long story of how our people have believed, behaved and worshipped from the beginning. As each of us receives the story we make it our own: now in our turn we hand it on. However, when we do so we have to remember that we are dealing with people who already have faith: faith which has grown and matured out of their experience of life, be they fifty-two, or twenty-seven, fifteen, or five years old. Therefore, when we share our own faith we have to meet and marry what we believe with the faith of other people:

— The people with whom we share our faith will already hold some of the beliefs and values we want to pass on: God is good; good will triumph; love is the most important of all values. All we do in this case is to invite them to reflect on what they hold and value in the light of our story.

— Some of our beliefs, values and symbols will spark off and tie in with and enrich experiences these people have had but never reflected on before. They find these beliefs and values we offer fulfilling and deeply satisfying.

— Some of our beliefs and values will clash with what they hold and cherish. To accept them means dislodging or purifying presently held values and beliefs or, in other words, being converted.

— And some of our beliefs and values will have no meaning for them at all. There is no way at this stage of their development that they can hear and make sense of some of the elements which we wish to share.

The following reflections I hope will begin to fill out what I have just said.

a. A GRACE-FILLED ACTIVITY

We live in a grace-filled world: sharing our faith is a graced activity. I like the comment in the *Rite of the Christian Initiation of Adults* which says the individual's spiritual journey 'varies according to the many forms of God's grace, the free cooperation of the individuals, the action of the church, and the circumstances of time and place' (RCIA 5). Be we evangelist, catechist, teacher, parent, priest, bishop, we are simply the instruments of the Holy Spirit: just as the Holy Spirit is the bond of love, so the Holy Spirit is the effectiveness of the ministry we exercise.

b. AFFIRMATION

The way we begin our faith-sharing is by exploring with others where they are on their faith-journey. We try to help them reflect on their lives and discover for themselves what gives meaning to their lives. Do they believe in God? What is their picture of God? Do they think God is interested in them? Is God creator? What do they think is important in life? Is love, friendship, loyalty, truth, important? How are these expressed in their lives? and in the lives of others? When are they happiest? What makes them afraid? What do they wish for? Whom and what do they trust? Thus we help them build up a picture for themselves of what they believe and value: we help them admit and own that these are their values and beliefs; and at the same time we offer affirmation: it is all right to hold this, there is nothing wrong, nothing to be ashamed of in being where you are on your journey. Thus we establish the base on which to build; and we offer them the necessary support and encouragement by building up their self-confidence.

This is just what parents are doing for their children. As the days, weeks and months go by they are continually affirming their children's belief in the triumph of good over evil and helping them understand it. They help them believe in themselves; they interpret their children's sense of wonder and mystery; and so they try to establish a meaningful and secure world for their children to live in.

c. FAITH BUILDS ON FAITH

The next point I can make clearer by using an example.

Bobby was a happy child; he came from a happy family. His mother was nominally a catholic: she did not go to church, nor did his father, who was not a catholic. His parents loved him and did their best to make his world safe and secure, banishing his fears and giving him self-confidence, thus helping him to make sense of his life. However, they rarely talked about God or anything religious. For reasons not specifically religious, his mother sent Bobby to a catholic school. There he met 'Miss'. 'Miss' was a very good, conscientious teacher; she was very worried because Bobby did not have any religion; she promptly taught him about God, Our Lady, creation, and how to say his prayers and what to do to be a 'good catholic'. 'Miss' gave Bobby religion. What she failed to do was to recognize what his parents had given him, and to marry the way he had begun to make sense of his world (that is his faith) with the religion she felt he needed and gave him. Because Bobby was only five years old the confusion in this pedagogy may not surface, but a tension has been created between what he receives from 'Miss' and his loving home: between faith and religion.

d. PERSONAL FAITH STORY

In the process of helping people understand their own present faith and values, it is good to get them to ask themselves whether they always thought as they do now: can they remember a time when they had different ideas and thought other things much more important? By asking them to look back at their lives, we help them to get in touch with their lives as a faith-journey and we help them discover what were the factors and the events which contributed to the development of their faith. As they come to understand their own faith-journey, so they see themselves as searching for the mystery at the heart of life. We can begin to give an understanding of faith as a journey quite simply, even to small children.

May I just develop this thinking with regard to children. I have been speaking of people getting in touch with what is going on in their lives so as to come to understand themselves with regard to their faith-journey and the values which are theirs. We must apply this also to children. Feelings play an enormous part in our lives and, therefore, from an early age children must be helped to handle them. Parents can ask them to name their feelings and say why they feel like that, so that they may learn how to trace where and when their feelings arose. Frequently children will need a lot of support to cope with their feelings, particularly negative ones, for example jealousy, loneliness, anger;

they will need assurance that it is alright to feel like that and how to learn from them. Indeed learning how to reflect in this way is a most important part of growing towards the next stage of the faith-journey.

The ability to reflect is at the heart of human experience;[18] it is in coming to terms with our experiences that we come to discern God present and at work in our lives. Furthermore, we can help children get in touch with faith as a journey simply by getting them to reflect on how they have changed over the years. What did they, for example, once quarrel about? Or what did they once dream of becoming when they were grown-up? This makes them realize how they have changed: nine year olds trying to remember what it was like when they were little. In doing this we are helping them to see that change is part of the process of growing and maturing which is the faith-journey. Also, in helping children get in touch with what they really believe and value, we discover that some of them have false ideas about religion; for example, a very poor or seriously false image of God. By listening to their story we may find out its cause: it may well have come about because of a bad relationship with their father. We are now in a position to offer remedial guidance.

e. CONTENT OF FAITH SHARING

This may be a systematic exploration of the truth of the faith in cate-chesis, a deeper exposition of the gospel in evangelisation or pre-senting some facet of religion in religious education. Whatever it is, I would like to introduce it by using the example of an adult would-be-convert to the church. Susan, the would-be-convert, approaches the church. She is seeking a way forward on her own faith-journey. The questions which she is asking of the church are: 'Have you got some-thing to offer me? Can you answer some of my questions?' The most helpful reply to these questions is not a system of beliefs nor an expo-sition of values, but for the christian (let us call him Luke) who meets her to say, 'I'll tell you how my christian faith helps me to make sense of my life', and then to share with her something of his own faith story.

The next step (I am simplifying the encounter for the sake of clarity) is for Luke to ask Susan to say why it is at this particular point in her life she is approaching the church. Susan replies by responding with

---

[18] See above, chapter 4, sections 1 and 2, p. 51.

her own faith story: how it has come about that she is now looking for answers to her questions about life. Now Luke, in listening to her story, is able to understand it in the light of his own faith-vision: he can discern the action of God in her life. He is able to understand various elements and movements in her life in the light of the christian story; he can begin to use words like love, forgiveness, goodness, the Holy Spirit, sin, and ideas like creation, redemption, resurrection which, as Susan tells her story, find echoes in her life. Luke, in fact, discovers that many beliefs and values central to the christian faith are already part of Susan's life. Then, as Luke continues to explore her story in the light of the gospel, Susan begins to get in touch with beliefs and values which at first are strange, perhaps uncomfortable for her and difficult to grasp. For example, she finds the gospel's understanding of forgiveness and its implications very challenging. It is then that she comes gradually to understand the cost of following Christ and embracing his kingdom.

Central to this encounter between Susan and Luke are the latter's efforts to help her see her life in the light of the gospel. This is true of all such encounters. When we try to help children, this is what we try to do. We encourage them to take their experiences of life, of love, dislike, happiness, failure, jealousy, excitement and look at them in the light of the gospel. Moreover, we help them to see that various aspects of the gospel are already present in their lives; what we are doing is helping them to build on those foundations.

f. A FEW RELATED IDEAS

This passage about Susan and Luke illustrates three points about sharing our faith, not just with adult would-be-converts, but with all our fellow pilgrims, be they adults or children:

- Sharing my faith produces echoes in the lives of those with whom I am sharing it: it ties in with, marries and illuminates their experience. An example to illustrate this would be speaking of the communal meal aspect of eucharist to one who has good experiences of family meals.

- Some of what I try to share will be new and strange, yet as I present it the person will reach towards it. The very presentation acts as an enabling factor in that person's life; my faith story touches off the action of the Spirit in the other's life.

— The third point is the connection between the faith-sharing and experience. As individuals grow up and mature and their experiences of personal relationships grow deeper, so they become progressively more able to integrate the christian story and make it part of their lives. The converse of what I am saying is equally important: there are certain aspects of faith-sharing which can only be shared according to the other person's understanding and appreciation of personal relationships. Some of it will be new, but will spark off experiences and help to illuminate them; the rest will be foreign, for which they may not yet be ready.

g. SHARING FAITH DEEPENS FAITH

Recently a mother said to me: 'I learnt more about God from my four-year-old son than I ever knew before.' Our faith-sharing is Spirit-filled. Have you ever had the experience of sharing a bright idea with a friend who responds by saying: 'Great, that is a good idea!' A pause ensues. Then he says: 'But have you thought of this . . ?' and he proceeds to say something which puts your idea into a completely new light, and helps you to see depths in what you said which you had not suspected were there. This is absolutely central to faith-sharing. We are not sharing an inert body of truth, but the living word of God, whose meaning and effectiveness does not belong to a closed system. Remember the words of Jesus: 'Well then, every scribe who becomes a disciple of the kingdom of heaven is like a householder who brings out from his storeroom things both new and old' (Matthew 13:52). We have, therefore, to be very sensitive to what our faith-sharing evokes in our hearers. Each one is unique; the Holy Spirit dwells in those with whom we share our faith. They hear what we say and they make it their own. Then we must be eager to hear what they make of it, how they can help us to deepen our own understanding of our faith.

h. LIFESTYLE

Faith-sharing also involves saying how I translate my faith into my daily living. Justice is an integral part of faith. The person of faith lives a life of justice. We have to discern with those with whom we share our faith how it should affect our lifestyle. This is not a simple question of embracing certain pious practices. It is allowing oneself to be challenged by the gospel. It involves a deep conversion to a life rooted in the beatitudes, and to a life in which prayer is at its heart.

i. FAITH AND VALUES

I would like here to make a slight detour and draw your attention to the relationship between beliefs and values. It is out of a people's basic beliefs that their values emerge. Because of my belief that God creates and shares God's self with every human being I honour and value the worth of every human being and respect the dignity of each. Because I believe passionately in the life, sufferings, death and resurrection of Jesus as the way of redemption, I can find a value in suffering, paradoxical though it may seem, and likewise come to appreciate that the meek will inherit the earth, the last will be first and that failure is not ultimate disaster. Thus beliefs give rise to values. There is, therefore, the closest relationship between beliefs and values. The problem in sharing faith with others often does not lie at the belief level but at the level of values. Our materialistic society offers a set of values which are frequently contradictory to that of the gospel and, in consequence, the values we attempt to offer do not speak to the lives of those we would like to influence. Take, for example, a class of highly intelligent and sophisticated fifteen-year-olds engrossed in exams, seeking good results in order to go eventually to universities and thence to the top of the ladder. What are their values? What exactly motivates their lives? Do their values actually form a basis, for example, on which they can be led to appreciate the eucharist? I am not saying that because of their intelligence and sophistication they do not have christian values: what I am saying is that we can only present the eucharist, which celebrates Christ's sacrificial life, death and resurrection, to those who live or want to live their lives in the light of the values it enshrines.

The norm of the good christian life is the life of Christ as expressed in the gospel: this is the ultimate criterion. Therefore, it goes without saying that christians make progress on their faith journeys as they follow Christ. Christians have to hold up each aspect of their lives to his light and discover the ways in which what they do, say and think are in harmony with his teaching and values. When we do this, we realize that there are undoubtedly aspects of our lives which do mirror Christ's life and some which are contrary. As we continue to make this kind of reflection we come to know not only about ourselves but also about the structures which hold our lives together. There are some things we can change, while others we simply have to tolerate because there is nothing we can do about them, they are so much part of the system in which we live. From early childhood we need to train children to reflect continually on what happens in their everyday lives, to hold up to the truth what they do, say and think, and learn to evaluate it.[19] In more adult terms, we are asking them to see in what ways they are trying to build the kingdom and what it is within them which is a counter-sign to that kingdom. Once this was called the Examination of Conscience. Today, spiritual writers use the term: Examination of Consciousness, making the point that it is equally important to appropriate the positive gospel aspects of our lives, as it is to be sorry for their negative aspects.

[19] See above, 'Personal faith story', p. 95.

Part Three

Settings

9

Community

In the last section I was dealing with how Christians share their faith. Logically, we must now consider the settings in which this takes place. What I am going to concentrate on are the home, the school and the parish; but before I do this I would like to reflect awhile on community, because community, in one way or another, affects what we do in these three settings.

1. Companionship

Human beings by nature are gregarious, although a number of them prefer their own company or find their need for other people satisfied by one or two friends. However, the majority feel a need for people and enjoy being with others. Some satisfy this need in working with others, some in sport, some in sharing a hobby, some in family life, some in their local pub: there is a vast variety of ways and places in which people come together and satisfy their need for companionship. Now the heart of companionship lies in the way we find ourselves accepted for what we are: we can be ourselves, we do not need to pretend, we can share our problems, we can build each other up. It is precisely this that the majority of us need. We need to be loved and cared for and, as a result, to exercise our own powers of loving and caring in return. Building people up, helping them to become more and more human, is God at work in us.

The Jerusalem Bible puts as a heading to chapter eighteen of Matthew, 'Discourse on the Church'. This chapter contains a series of related pieces about how people are to get on with one another, and it makes much of forgiveness (repent and believe the good news) as central to the way they live and work together and become Church. It is in this context that the evangelist, reflecting on the way people relate to one another, puts Jesus' saying: 'For where two or three meet in my name, I shall be there with them' (Matthew 18:20). In the light of the mystery of the risen Christ the church, reflecting on God's presence and action within people, expresses her understanding of it in this way: 'Where is love and loving kindness, God is fain to dwell', which is but an elaboration of John's, 'God is love and anyone who lives in love lives in God, and God will live in him' (I John 5:16). We believe, therefore, that all true companionship is the work of God, whether or not those who make up the company acknowledge God.

The very word 'companionship' takes us to the heart of human relationships. The word 'companionship' is made up from latin words which mean 'sharing bread together'. We come together to share and in sharing we deepen our understanding of one another, and thus we are drawn closer to one another into a oneness. Jesus' teaching continually emphasises the importance of oneness and he places it as the climax of his prayer for us to the Father: 'Father, may they be one in us, as you are in me and I am in you, so that the world may believe it was you who sent me' (John 17:21). The achieving of this unity was going to be no easy thing: his praying for it showed it was God's gift: it would only be attained in the fullness of God's kingdom.

In companionship we, therefore, struggle towards living together in peace, truth, love and justice, towards the oneness to which we are all called. Companionship. . . .

- expresses our need for one another as human beings: I need you and you need me

- takes us out of our loneliness and helps us to fulfil our need of one another

- offers us a means of belonging to and being accepted by others, which gives us a sense of personal significance and value

- accepts us as we are: we are valued simply for what we are and not for what we achieve

- enables us to grow and develop and supports us, not only in our attempts to deepen our relationships, but in all our enterprises

— enables us to build others up: through being loved and cared for ourselves, we are enabled to love, respect, value, and support others; and this leads us to a deep sense of solidarity.

2. Community?

Companionship is the heart of community. What I have been saying about companionship characterises community. As with companionship so with community, it is something we experience rather than define. We know to what extent we have achieved community by the quality of the relationships which are present among us and how we function as an entity. There are two possible extremes in people coming together: on the one hand they join together in order to do something but they barely tolerate one another; or, on the other hand, and this is the greater danger, in coming together they form a little world of their own, a closed society and are bound to one another by an unhealthy love which erects barriers between itself and the outside world: they become an élite.[20]

3. Basic communities

In recent years the church has been feeling its way forward in South America by encouraging the establishment and development of basic communities as, perhaps, the main instrument of its pastoral strategy. There, people — mainly the very poor — have come together to reflect upon their experiences of life in the light of the gospel, in the face of the injustices inherent in countries where the vast proportion of the land and the country's wealth is in the hands of a rich and powerful minority.

— They come together out of a sense of need for one another to meet a common threat

— they become united through sharing together the experience of being poor and unjustly treated

[20] Cults are examples of élitism. They almost always violate individual freedom.

- they find a way forward through holding up their daily experiences of life to the light of the gospel and in so doing find the presence of Christ among them

- more often than not they can change little of the real situation in which they live, but what they do accomplish is a growing sense of their dignity as human beings, an ever deepening solidarity, a sense of personal value and significance, and a mutual, felt involvement in each other's sufferings.

The context of our lives is very different in Europe and I am not suggesting that we simply lift the South American experience of basic communities and translate it as such into our own christian lives. What I think we need to learn from it is to value community as a real pastoral instrument.

4. Parish

We often speak of the parish community, but the parish can probably be no more than a loose gathering of very many different groups of people. The eucharist is pre-eminently the sign of true community. There, christians partake of the body and blood of Christ to become one body, filled with the Spirit of the Lord. It is the sign of what they are striving to become and which they have not yet attained. It does not follow, therefore, that every gathering of God's people at their parish Mass is necessarily a true community. The circumstances in which they gather, the diversity of those who gather and the variety in their kinds of commitment, preclude a sense of significance and solidarity inevitably resulting. What we can say is, and this is very important, the eucharist calls and enables God's pilgrim people to become community. As for the people who gather for Sunday Mass, so for the parish as a whole; it does not have those characteristics which are the hallmark of community: its very size, alongside its diversity, does not make it a place where people can feel themselves closely bound to one another and enjoy through this solidarity a deep sense of affirmation and acceptance. Perhaps the parish, as it presently exists, can never be more than a gathering of communities: I hesitate to use the phrase, 'a community of communities.'

5. Groups versus community

In a parish we have groups like St Vincent de Paul, Union of Catholic Mothers, a youth group, a justice and peace group, a liturgy group, parent groups, a prayer group: any of these groups may or may not be community. This depends on the amount individuals are willing to invest of themselves in each other and in achieving the aim of that group. There is a close link between a strong commonfelt desire for some goal which individuals make great efforts to achieve and the quality of relationships which develop among them: this is what changes a group into a community. A friend of mine reluctantly began to attend some parish meetings about her daughter's first holy communion; she thought this was totally unnecessary: this was the job of the school. Her reluctance turned into resentment when she was put into a small group of parents and asked to share with the other parents what she felt about holy communion. The lady at her right spoke first and my friend was so astonished by what she heard about that lady's struggle to make any real sense of holy communion at all, that her resentment gave way to a desire to tell the lady what it was all about, only to discover that her own pat answers were firmly rejected and she found herself completely lost. There was never any doubt about her returning to the other meetings. 'I suddenly realized I needed these people. It was never enough to read the books or listen to the priest; I had to discover what it meant to other people.' The group began to have a life of its own through becoming involved in their children's first communion, through sharing their personal experiences and eventually learning how to reflect on those experiences in the light of the gospel. They did, in fact, become community.

Community, I said above, is something one experiences rather than defines. It sounds almost trite to say that suddenly one realizes that something has happened to this group of oddly assorted people and they have become an entity with a life of their own; and with that life a purpose and an incredible strength. There are very many groups of people who call themselves community because they enjoy a certain ease and conviviality among themselves, but this is not of itself the essence of community. I believe true and deep community always has a dimension which reflects that something greater has happened to these individuals than simply an amalgamation of their individual strengths and abilities warrant; this is the fruit of the way they mutually enrich one another by sharing among themselves their experiences of life and their own felt needs.

It is this mutual sharing which characterises the dimension I spoke about above which leads to action, to a sense of being able to achieve together something for themselves; but it will also necessarily lead them to be concerned about others beyond their own community. I think it is possible to see this in the determination of certain people concerned with peace or ecology, for example. In specifically christian settings members of communities turn instinctively to the gospels and review their experiences and needs in their light; the light which of its nature gives life to what they do.

6. Summary

I hope by now I have said enough to introduce you to community as a pastoral tool, and help you to see how effective an instrument it could be. I would like to leave you with the following summary:

● Community can emerge among people who come together to achieve something or to meet a common threat. For example, parents involved in their children's first communion, old people looking for ways to improve their conditions and find companionship, young people faced with unemployment, parishioners concerned with street violence or bad housing or poor race relations, single parent families seeking mutual support.

● Community can be identified as community by the quality of relationships which develop among the members: an atmosphere of mutual support, interest and encouragement emerges, based on the acceptance of common christian values:

— members acquire a sense of personal significance through the way they are accepted, respected and listened to

— members develop a sense of solidarity through belonging to a community which leads them to acknowledge their need of one another

— members feel free and secure to share their personal experiences; a sense of trust develops and with it members feel they can be themselves, say what they think and not to have to pretend; their relationships are deeply compassionate

- members can feel their way to self-fulfilment as together they explore what is life-giving and leads to a deeper grasp of what is genuinely human

- members' individual concern for the young unemployed, for example, is deepened and sharpened and rendered effective: together they may do something about it

- members come to see that as they share their personal experiences they are sharing God's action in their lives: and they come to see their need as a group to hold up these experiences to the light of the gospel and to prayer

- members, while they are conscious of having been formed into a community because of some particular personal need or to accomplish a particular task, come to see themselves as offering a service to the larger community and to society. Moreover, they make themselves ready to receive new members and resist the temptation to become elitist.

7. Settings

I have just been talking about community as a setting for faith-sharing. In the next three chapters, I will go on to look at home, parish and school, not so much as communities but as places for faith-sharing.

I am using faith-sharing to include catechesis, evangelisation, and religious education. May I remind you what I mean. I know there are times when I find it very helpful to talk over my faith with another believer *(catechesis):* I am aware that I continually require the power of the gospel to transform my materialistic tendencies *(evangelisation);* and there are times when I need to explore the whole area of the meaning of life, and, discover what it is that governs my own and other people's lives *(religious education).* Finally, may I add *evangelising-catechesis* which, I hope, speaks for itself and is perhaps the most common kind.

10

Home

1. Ideals

I feel that there is a great danger, when we come to discuss this subject, of simply making bland cosmetic statements. We can read again and again of the home as the 'domestic church', of children being wrapped in the expressive faith context of their parents, and can agree that faith is not so much taught as caught; caught within the faith-life of the family. Now, while this is undoubtedly true, 'things seldom accord with the ideal'.

I know a man of Catholic parents whose earlier years were marked with a constant stream of family violence, whose parents broke up at the end of his childhood and whose inner life was marred as a result, but whose memory also recalls a whole stream of Catholic practices weaving in and out of the unhappiness and tensions of childhood: this man still struggles whole-heartedly with his faith-journey. There is a woman I know, whose infancy and childhood were marked by unimaginable lovelessness, including abuse, who now struggles to lead a very harmonious, dedicated christian life. But there is David, whose family background and upbringing could be used by a Catholic family textbook to illustrate all its ideals but now, as he drifts along smilingly, has no apparent religious affiliation at all.

I am sure that the examples I have just given remind you of similar ones: you can cap each one and add others of your own. It seems to me, therefore, if this section is to ring true, we must focus very sharply on the reality of family as it is being experienced as the twentieth century moves towards its conclusion; and, as we bring our focus into relief, a very disheartening picture is revealed. But, to begin with, I would like first to explore and highlight some of the positive ideals of marriage and family.

Again and again speakers draw our attention to the mounting divorce rate and the consequent erosion of family life, with alarm and sadness. 'The Family as an Institution is under Threat!' This, however, is not quite true, because many divorced people re-marry and set up another family, and even after a second divorce some make a third attempt. There is something so enormously attractive in living together in loving closeness with another human being that the individual will struggle to achieve it, once, twice, three times . . . To have the felt experience of being loved completely and totally, and striving to respond and return that love, is the highest of human achievements: and this must be so if we take St John's first letter seriously'.

> God is love
> . . . as long as we love one another
> God will live in us,
> and his love will be complete in us.
>   (1 John 4:8 and 12)

Husbands and wives give themselves to each other: they put their hearts in each other, (to put one's heart is to believe and struggle to live out their mutual commitment). And God, in a phrase very familiar to us, is really and truly present in the depths of their hearts whether they know it or not, and still less whether they are able to name it in theological or religious language.

This mutual self-giving is the most important thing in the faith-life of every husband and wife: it is precisely their love for each other which is central to the way in which they find meaning for themselves and make sense of the world. Christians not only enjoy what all married people who are striving to live a life of love enjoy, but out of their Christian heritage are able to name what is happening in their lives, share their understanding of it with their fellow christians and celebrate and purify it in their regular eucharists; and in this way are ready to offer those who do not accept their christian beliefs something of the richness contained in the christian story about marriage. I am stressing this quotation from St John's first letter because most children begin their lives in a loving context. A relationship is established: parents give themselves knowingly and willingly to their babies, desiring to love them into existence; and there is a corresponding response to this love in their children. It is deep within this relationship that the faith journey begins, not just for children from a family which has an avowed religious commitment, but for every child; not just for babies whose parents can name God's presence and action in their babies' lives, but for all babies.

2. Today's family

Here I want to look at the experiences of married family life at the point we have reached in the twentieth century. To do this I begin with the rather stark predictions of an American organization involved in life insurance.

It will not be uncommon, says the report, for children born in the eighties to follow this sequence of living arrangements:[21]

> live with both parents for several years
> live with their mothers after their parents' divorce
> live with their mothers and stepfathers
> live alone for a time in their early twenties
> live with someone of the opposite sex without marrying
> get married
> get divorced
> live alone again or with children
> get remarried
> and end up living alone again following the death of their spouse.

Clearly, this pattern will have many permutations and combinations. Technologically advanced nations today are honeycombed with a bewildering array of family forms. There are contract marriages, serial marriages, family clusters, and a variety of intimate networks with or without shared sex. No less than 86 different combinations of adults, including different forms of 'mother-grandmother' families, 'mother-father families', and 'mother-other' families were uncovered in a poor area of a major American city.[22]

---

[21] I am indebted to 'The shape of the American Family in the Year 2000', Trend Analysis Program 1982, Fall Issue, American Council of Life Insurance.

[22] Toffler, Alvin, *The Third Wave*, Collins, 1980.

Of the situation in our own country today, as it touches our immediate subject, we are faced with:

● The majority of catholics do not marry other catholics. Mixed marriages are the norm.

● The divorce rate continues to rise. One result of this is the growing number of single-parent families. Although the children of such families suffer an obvious deprivation, nevertheless many of these families are extremely well-adjusted. However, single parents are very restricted socially and can become very isolated, especially during the infancy and childhood of their children.

● Unemployment is becoming a way of life in some areas: not only are many of the young people unemployed but also their fathers have never had regular employment. The struggle and strains of continuing unemployment can be extremely difficult for family life. A growing number of girls with no employment prospects, for example, will have babies simply to get away from the family home and live on state-provided benefits.

● The demands of industry require a highly mobile work force: the consequences of this policy mean that many young families live at a considerable distance from both sets of parents, and without the friendships of their early years. These families lack that very necessary support-network which they need in early married life and, although they may be establishing new networks of their own, these are no substitute for the tried, rooted patterns of kinship families.

● Consumerism, along with the success ethic, can eat away at the heart of family life by creating a whole area of dissatisfaction within the intimacy of that life.

● The increase in drug-taking, both among parents and children, points to their inability to cope with life.

● Similarly, parents are frequently faced with their children's delinquency and violence, straining family life.

● Finally, a study has just been published on 'Values and Social

Change in Britain'. I think the conclusions at the end of the chapter on the family are well worth considering. I quote them directly as they are printed:

Conclusions

This chapter [of the report] began by looking at some of the prevailing stereotypes of marriage and family life, e.g. beliefs that these institutions are being undermined by some of the more strident aspects of feminism or that there is an increase in single parenthood, or that the young are rejecting marriage. The research literature and empirical data from the Values Survey, however, indicates that the institutions themselves are not under threat but rather changes have taken place in the ways that individuals live out their marital and family lives.

Certainly it is the common expectation amongst young people that they will be married. The Values Survey data showed that 84% of those questioned disagreed with the statement that marriage was an outdated institution.

It is not the fact of marriage that is being questioned, but rather the quality of married life. Despite the increase in the divorce rate there is also an increase in remarriage. Twenty years ago Berger Kellner (1964) wrote:

Individuals in our society do not divorce because marriage has become unimportant to them, but because it has become so important that they have no tolerance for the less than completely successful marital arrangement.

In other words, although increasing numbers of people are rejecting specific marriage partners, the institution of marriage is not threatened and this is underlined by the high rate of re-marriage following divorce. It seems, too, that women are not only more dissatisfied with the quality of married life, but also increasingly take the initiative in trying to put things right or even dissolve the relationship.

There is a high degree of consensus from those taking part in the Values Study of the factors thought to contribute to successful marriage, i.e. faithfulness, mutual respect and understanding and tolerance. There is a high level of satisfaction with home life with more of those espousing traditional values reporting being happy and satisfied with home life than holding either transitional or post-traditional values.[23]

Those holding traditional views are more likely to think that drunkenness, violence or unfaithfulness are not sufficient grounds for divorce. As views move away from the traditional these factors are seen as unacceptable within the marriage.

There is also evidence from the study that those perceiving they had strict parents report not only being closer to but also sharing more values with both their parents and marriage partners. Irrespective of global value orientation, parents wish to impart the values of honesty, tolerance, respect and good manners to their children. The importance of children's wellbeing is paramount with a total of 72% of respondents believing it is the duty of parents to do their best for their children even at the expense of their own wellbeing.

In both attitudes and behaviour, the respondents to the Values Study showed little evidence of departing radically from traditional views of either family or marriage. Over two-thirds felt a child needs a home with both a father and a mother; less than 2% said they were living as married, more women with dependent children stayed at home than went out to work and dual career families (i.e. wives following a professional career) are still in the minority.

It can, therefore, be concluded that the so-called cereal packet model of family life is still the norm for most families. There is strong support for marriage: the presence of both parents for their children's wellbeing; agreement that the setting of that wellbeing should be within a family of two or possibly three children; finally, it was evident that similar values are handed on from parents to children. Global value orientation seem to be less of a reaction against but rather a continuation of values shared with parents.[24]

[23] In an earlier chapter of the report, Mark Abrams describes a typology of value systems. Those holding *traditional* views tend to be older, married or widowed. *Transitionalists* are more likely to be in the 35-54 age group whilst the *post-traditionalists* more often fall within the 18-34 age group. Being younger the latter are also more frequently represented amongst the single. Class as such did not differentiate people in terms of these global values. When looking at the relative satisfaction with home life, certainly married women are less satisfied than married men, and housewives with dependent children are the least satisfied.

[24] Taken from, Chapter 5, 'Marriage and Family', J. Brown, M. Comber, K. Gibson, S. Howard, 1984, in *Values and Social Change in Britain*, A report of the European Value System Study Group, edited by Mark Abrams, David Gerard, Noel Timms.

3. Family: faith-sharing

What emerges from the last section is that while there are innumerable problems besetting the family today, people set great store by family life and appreciate its values and possibilities. In fact, it is clearly indicated that one reason for the increase in divorce is that people are seeking a better family life. This longing for a richer family life is rooted deep within ourselves in our desire for love and companionship. We know that this is the ideal setting for children to grow in faith. The gospels offer a vision of life, of how we should live together: making love, forgiveness, compassion, truth, honesty, respect central to all our relationships. Here I have attempted to translate the gospel vision into questions we can ask ourselves about our family. I am sure these questions will make you think of many more. We are here once more touching upon the kingdom vision of life which Jesus proclaimed, and which is at the heart of the story we have received and to which we must bear witness.

— Do the members of the family enjoy one another's company?

— Are there genuine expressions of real affection?

— Can all the members of the family be themselves without having to pretend?

— Can each one expect and receive help and support in what he/she is doing? Do all take each other's troubles to heart?

— Do they all express real interest in one another's doings while still allowing each his/her own privacy?

— Do they feel a sense of solidarity? Do they really feel they belong to one another?

— How does the family cope with the wrong-doing of a member?

— Do they all experience real forgiveness after wrong-doing? Is the wrong completely forgotten or are they regularly reminded of it?

— How does the family tackle the question of prayer?

— Are the talents of each member discovered and developed?

- Is each one given an opportunity to talk about himself/herself and his/her doings? Is each one listened to?

- Does the family offer a refuge at a time of failure? Are individuals given the opportunity to talk about their faith?

- Do all the members rejoice at each other's successes? Do they try to appreciate what success is in one another's lives?

- Are all the members involved in some degree in family decisions?

- In making a decision to acquire an expensive item for the house, on what principles does the family operate?

- Are family meals a chore or enjoyable occasions?

- Is the family concerned in welcoming friends into their home? each other's friends?

- How does the family cope with aging relatives?

- What are the main qualities you would look for in a school to which to send your children?

- Are you involved in your children's school?

4. Family: scope and limitations

The family, unquestionably, is universally acknowledged to be the key factor in the formation and development of our faith; but, having said that, it is important to acknowledge also its limitations. Put it this way: from one point of view our parents are our best teachers; we learn more from them about life than from any other human being. Yet from another point of view, there are some areas of learning which are dealt with better by people outside the family circle. There is something about the closeness of family life which to some extent inhibits formal teaching, if not always, certainly for very definite periods in children's development. This 'something' is to do with authority. The family does have an authority of its own, but it is an authority which coexists with love, intimacy and familiarity, and thus provides a basis for trust and security. It is of a different kind from the authority which children need in order to validate certain issues or areas they wish to come to understand. There are occasions when children need an authority outside the family. They need the reassurance that this is more than 'Mum doing her own thing?' or 'Just Dad on his hobby horse!'

We need also to consider here a further point. We have seen that when we talk about 'handing on the faith' we mean initiating individuals into the christian story: now the family by itself simply has not got the resources to do this; the christian story is much greater than the family. If the family were made the central and essential place for communicating the faith to another generation, there would indeed be serious danger of privatising the message and clericalising the family. Help to hand on the christian story is needed from others: friends, teachers, catechists, priests, etc. particularly in providing children with a more formal catechesis.

Obviously parents play an important part in their children's faith-life; this we noted in introducing this section. They set the scene; provide the content for growth; shield their children from influences they are not capable of combating, yet give them the freedom they need to develop personal responsibility; draw their children into their own religious practices; introduce them to the parish community; talk to them about what they believe. But I am convinced that they can only do this provided the families are supported by a christian fellowship which is both larger (and hence more public) than the family, and smaller (and hence more intimate) than the local parish community. Families need support from family groups, parents' meetings, groups of friends, etc. The church does not begin in the family. It begins in the community; it is the job of pastoral planning to welcome the family and to make it feel a part of the local community.

11

School

I now want to look at the school as a setting for faith-sharing. The questions to be answered are: Why have catholic schools at all? What are their aims and objectives?

1. The achievement and the challenge

With the Foster Education Act of 1870 the hierarchy of England and Wales threw their episcopal energies into creating a catholic education system as the principal means of building up a catholic community in England and Wales. In doing this the bishops were eminently successful. Catholics became an established part of the life of England and Wales, with catholic doctors, lawyers, members of parliament, professors, writers and teachers. The church in this country created an educated catholic laity in less than fifty years.

The model catholic school was the 'all-age' school situated alongside the church; it catered for the children of the parish and was staffed by teachers who lived in the parish: the whole complex was presided over by the parish priest. There were no doubts about the purpose of this school: its aim was to produce good practising catholics. Catholic boys were to marry catholic girls, whose children would be baptised in the parish church. This was an age when mixed marriages were performed secretly in the sacristy.

Two world wars, the Education Act of 1944 and a theological revolution summed up in the Second Vatican Council, have made us think again about many things; what are the aims of catholic schooling, at least as far as this country is concerned? I add the qualification 'this country', because I am not referring so much to catholic educational theory as such, but rather to the pragmatic situation which has developed among us.

Quite clearly the catholic school system was developed to complement the catholic home; the teachers were *in loco parentis:* catholic teachers used their professional educational expertise to do what catholic parents could not. A catholic world was created for the children to grow up in, a world sheltered from alien influences, among which protestantism probably figured more seriously than materialism. Be that as it may, the spirituality governing the whole process of 'handing on the faith' strongly stressed isolationism, 'to keep oneself pure and unspotted from the world' (and other religions). We have here strong echoes of the cloister and the convent, and even stronger ones of the church as the One Ark of Salvation — the Barque of Peter: 'No salvation outside the church'. One's faith was something one needed to guard and protect. Moreover those who did have to become involved in the world would find in the church a place to renew themselves and deepen their grasp of christian values. The school, therefore, along with the parish church and the home, were components of the Ark. What the church had created in the midst of society, which was in part protestant and in part secular and materialistic, was a closed community, anxious about its identity and self-preservation.

2. Second Vatican Council

For the sake of presenting this argument it would be neat to be able to say: 'Well, of course, the Second Vatican Council changed all that!' But it didn't! The Council set itself the slow, arduous task of renewing the church in the light of its tradition (the church's story) and in view of its mission to transform society. It engaged itself in the delicate task of making the church part of the society to which it wished to give the gospel.

In the Council documents we have a rich quarry of theological reflections. Here I simply want to remind you of some ideas which bear upon what I am saying:

- God is present and working within the life of every single member of human-kind — loving each one, not just into existence and preserving each; but loving each one into salvation.

— As Jesus is God's gift to the world, so is the church God's gift to human-kind. As Jesus came among the people of his day, serving them and meeting their needs, so likewise today does the church. Her vocation is to care not just for her own members but for everyone.

3. Tension

A tension arises between catechesis and evangelisation: on the one hand opportunities for deepening faith are needed (nurture), while on the other hand there must be opportunities for conversion. There is no easy answer to this tension. Three things need to be said:

a. The church exists in order to evangelise: she achieves her deepest identity in evangelising (cf. *Evangelium Nuntiandi* 14). Evangelisation is directed not only towards those who do not claim to belong to her, but also towards her own members.

b. Catechesis, since it involves faith-sharing, can only be done in a faith-community; among believers. We shall see directly whether or not a school really fulfils the definition of a faith-community.

c. Growth in faith takes place, not only by living in a faith community, but equally in the process of serving the needs of others and evangelising them. We grow in holiness by working for the kingdom.

4. We have sinned!

In meeting many catholics today who are involved in one way or another with schools (teachers, priests, laity, bishops), I sense an enormous amount of guilt and frustration. The all-age parish school broods heavily over the whole scene. 'Why aren't our catholic schools producing good practising catholics?' Statistics (though reliable ones are hard to come by) seem to indicate a tremendous drop in mass attendance. 'Children today just don't know the faith as we did!' 'They don't go to confession!' 'They're all so free and easy today: there's no discipline.' 'It's all so airy-fairy.' Today the catholic school is made to take the blame for every ill.

Perhaps one of the most poignant cries runs something like this: the catholic community in England and Wales made enormous sacrifices to produce the catholic school system in order to build itself up:

> 'Look at the vast sums of money we found. We had a dream about there being more and more catholics, more and more parishes, more and more priests and nuns, more and more of our fellow-countrymen becoming catholic and we dreamt we would exercise more and more influence in the running of our country. Our prayers for the conversion of England and Wales have not been granted. Where did we go wrong? We have sinned! We are guilty!'

My first reaction to this is, 'Yes, we are guilty.' It is for our faults that we are punished. We should have kept ourselves to ourselves: emphasised the catholic community, made people go to Mass, resisted the demise of the parish school, kept non-catholic pupils and teachers out of our system, fought more vigorously the attractiveness of our consumer society, attacked the state in its efforts to standardise our system, resisted the pressures to achieve as good or better exam results in the name of catholicism than the state or public school system, made much greater efforts to keep the catholic faith pure and untainted in our schools . . . My litany of recriminations can go on and my guilt towers higher than my head.

However, I have a feeling that things aren't as simple as that! Guilt is a thing we should avoid and get rid of as quickly as possible.

Before anything else, however, we must pay tribute to the vision of our catholic forebears and the enormous sacrifices which they made to implement that vision through the catholic school system; and given the continuance of the kind of society and culture in which it germinated and flowered, it could well have produced the harvest they had in mind. But the 'given' did not come off.

5. Change

I am no sociologist and I do not want to dabble in areas which are outside my competence. All I can do here is to suggest that you consult the relevant authorities who reflect and comment on the vast changes which took place in our society after the second world war, and in particular during the sixties, which some of those authorities label the Expressive Revolution. I suppose what strike me as key factors are a new understanding of authority, the emphasis placed on the individual and the growth of personalism along with a sudden growth in prosperity. A vast number of new products came on the market. Television became part of the national scene.

Thus the society in which we lived as catholics and which we were seeking to influence and convert by means of our catholic school system underwent a revolution; a revolution which also penetrated both the lives of catholics as they were caught up in it and the school system we had built. Earlier on I spoke of how the individual's faith-journey moves along as it is challenged by the events of life.[25] Loss of a job, sickness, a breakdown in relationships, make people think again and reshape their faith. Likewise a community is called through crisis to reflect upon its faith-commitment and the ways it adopts to share its faith story. This is part of our experience of growth and development as a church.

6. Where we are: Now!

We need, therefore, to look at the situation which has grown up around us and then begin to use our wit to discover what is demanded of us today:

● A small proportion of the children in our schools come from fully committed catholic backgrounds. A similar proportion is there for all sorts of reasons other than religion. The reasons why some parents send their children to catholic schools are very varied. There are educational and disciplinary reasons: many catholic schools have excellent reputations in these areas. There are geographical reasons: it is 'next door'.

● The percentage of mixed marriages has been running at about 70% now for some considerable time.

● The number of children from single-parent families is very signifi-

---

[25] See above, chapter 7, section 1, 'Growing faith', p. 76.

cant: in certain inner city areas, it could be as high as 33%. I offer this as a fact to be considered. Many single-parent families are however extremely happy, stable well-adjusted families.

● Only a few years ago the number of non-catholic pupils in our maintained schools would not have been considered significant; now in some schools this is changing. In the maintained sector in 1984 the overall average of non-catholics was low, about 7%, but there is a growing number of startling exceptions. In the independent sector which accounts for 10% of our schools (but under 9% of all the children in catholic schools), the number of non-catholics is about 45%: there are more non-catholic girls than catholic girls in the independent sector.

● On 15 October 1984, the Report of the Working Party on Catholic Education in a Multiracial, Multicultural Society was published (*Learning from Diversity: A Challenge for Catholic Education*). The report argues that 'the experience of a racially mixed school is a richer educational experience than that of a predominantly white school'. This statement touches some of the underlying assumptions of the Report: what is our education system offering to pupils of different races and cultures? Factually we have one maintained primary school which is 20% catholic and 80% Moslem (1984).

● Varying degrees of commitment appear among the teachers in our catholic schools. Some teachers make no contribution to the religious life of the school apart from that which follows on from their professional duties, while others are deeply involved both in and out of school.

● An average of about 35% of all the teachers in our comprehensive schools are non-catholics: this varies regionally from about 12% to over 50%. The picture is very different in the primary schools, where the number of non-catholic teachers is not nationally significant.

● The percentages above refer to the maintained sector. With regard to independent primary schooling the percentage of non-catholic teachers is about 27%, while the independent secondary sector does not differ greatly from the maintained sector. As a postscript it should be noted that a much higher percentage of religious, both men and women, who are full-time teachers are found to be in the independent sector than in the maintained sector: one religious for every 512 pupils in the maintained sector and one for every 87 pupils in the independent sector. With regard to graduate religious the corresponding figures are 1:1392 and 1:189.

Here I am simply recording the fact that over the years we have invited a significant number of non-catholic teachers into our schools.

● Primary schools are attached to parishes; and the parish priest is generally the chairperson of the Board of Governors. He, or an assistant priest, is involved in the religious needs of the children.

● Comprehensive schools serve many parishes and, though one of the local priests is frequently the chairperson of the Board of Governors, the relationship between the local clergy and the pupils is very loose. Many of these schools have a chaplain, in some cases part-time; some of the chaplains are religious sisters.

● Religious education is taught by most of the members of a primary school staff.

● Most comprehensive schools do have at least one religious education specialist, and in some cases this person heads a trained religious education staff.

7. Gospel versus materialism

These, therefore, are the main factors we have to deal with when we come to ask ourselves, 'What is the purpose of a catholic school in today's world?' And, in order to discover this purpose, perhaps the most urgent question we have to address is: How are we to present the gospel to the society in which we live? How are we to offer an enriching vision of life?

There is no easy answer, because the gospel in which we seek to root the life of our catholic schools opposes a materialistic world which has no place for the divine dimension. The confrontation between the gospel and this world makes itself felt nowhere more acutely than within the life of the school, which continually has to function between an ethic which sets great store on personal achievement as the road to success, and one based on the gospel which speaks of the first being last and the last being first. This tension is incredibly difficult to handle, because the people involved are mainly of exceptional good will who are continually struggling to form a new generation of human beings. 'Well, of course, I accept what you say and if I had only myself to consider I would have no problem but I have to think about my child. How can I impose my views on another human being? How can I not offer him a chance of success?' This kind of agonising is part of the daily life of very many parents, whose own lives are caught up in the necessity to live and maintain their standard of living.

We live in a society in which success is measured in monetary terms. There are enormous pressures on a young person to do well at school, to get good results, to get a good job. Inevitably in such a system, exam results are packaged with a price-tag. Learning has become a consumer product. High among the qualities parents look for in evaluating a school comes the school's place in the league of exam results. Harsh this may sound but parents, like the school, are caught up in a system over which they have little control.

The tragedy of this system for the many who are not successful is failure. Success breeds failure. This ethic uses expressions about the successful such as, 'They deserve to get on,' which presupposes that the others do not; and herein lies the injustice. Biblical justice struggles to meet people in their needs, to give to each what each needs to reach his/her own unique fullness.

8. The educated person

Whatever may be the reality, we all have some idea of what we really mean by education as an ideal. I do not want here to enter into a long discussion on the nature of education, but simply to evoke in your imagination certain ideals connoted by terms such as 'the educated man/woman' or 'a person of culture'. They bring to my mind individuals who certainly possess a broad spectrum of knowledge but also a deep understanding of people and events, a great tolerance of humankind and a quality which we use the word 'humanity' to describe. Now it is precisely this understanding of education which in theory the christian tradition has always upheld and has vigorously defended, especially when accused of being anti-intellectual.

What christianity has always promoted is an education which leads to the fullness of being human: its contribution to education is an understanding of what it means to be human, which it derives from the gospel entrusted to it. Jesus is human: if we want to know what we are educating children to become, we need to have ever in our minds the Christ of the gospel. I know that in saying this I am saying nothing new: we have always said our aim is to produce 'other Christs', but I believe this ideal somehow or other lost its thrust in a confused understanding of Jesus.

In our past presentation of Jesus we always stressed his divinity, and in so doing under-emphasised how human he was. We put Jesus out of reach of everyday life; we felt a need to filter his words and deeds in order to put them in realistic terms for our daily lives. To believe that Jesus is expressing a human reality in what he said and did and in the values he espoused, that he is the realistic expression of what it is to be human, challenges us to the depth of our being. This is, however, what we are asserting; and it is this concept of what it means to be a human being that we are offering the society in which we live: a society rooted in materialism.

9. Vision of life

In its schools, therefore, the church struggles to offer a gospel vision of life: a vision based on her understanding of what it is to be human, derived from pondering the mystery of Christ in the gospels. In doing this the church is being church in this school. The church is being true to her identity: the church exists in order to evangelise. To evangelise means to take the Good News into the lives of all, offering them a way to live and enjoy life to the full. She evangelises when she seeks to convert solely through the divine power of the message she proclaims; to convert the hearts of individuals, of groups and of nations; to transform, by means of the values of the gospel people's lives, what they do and the society of which they are part, thereby overturning materialistic criteria of judging and evaluating, lines of thinking, and models of life which are contrary to God's saving work. The vision is challenging and breathtaking. It is talking, not simply of the conversion of individuals to a gospel life, but of the conversion of the collective conscience of materialistic society to embrace the kingdom, as Jesus presents it to human-kind through the instrumentality of the church. (Cf. *Evangelisation in the Modern world:* Apostolic Exhortation, Paul VI, 14, 18, 19.)

I have elsewhere discussed the kingdom as a vision of life and society in which all the nations of the world: men, women, children and families of every race, colour and culture live together in peace, truth, justice and charity, sharing the earth's goods, valuing the whole of creation, the mountains, trees, fields, rivers and the animals, and respecting and sharing the earth's resources. It is a vision, a dream, which Jesus, at the head of the line of Old Testament prophets, proposed to the people of his day and which he entrusted to his church. Christianity has this vision, this future and the assurance that with the power of the Spirit nothing is impossible. It is this kingdom ideal which is central to church and, therefore, to the catholic school. It is this alternative way of living which we try to demonstrate through the way we run our schools.

And so we come to the crux: how do we translate the gospel into the everyday life of the school? how can the gospel transform the school's structures and system? what methodology do we adopt so that the gospel is enabled to exercise its transforming power on the lives of the individual pupils?[26]

10. Vision and daily life

Pupils are evangelised simply by living among people whose lives are deeply affected by the values of the gospel and who endeavour to let these values permeate the structures which hold their lives together.

> — Is there a place for complete forgiveness in our schools? Do you know of occasions when pupils have done something quite seriously wrong and have been completely forgiven and the incident never referred to again? Are pupils really enabled to live their pasts down?

[26] To evangelise is to convert, to come to have that mind which was in Christ Jesus (Phil 2:5); that is, to rule one's life by his attitudes and his values.

Evangelisation is a life-long process; before catechesis can be given to individuals they must at least desire to have the mind of Christ. Many teachers give catechesis before they have really attempted to face the pagan reality of their pupils' lives.

— Do our schools really try to keep their disruptive pupils? or do they take the earliest opportunity to rid themselves of them?

— Do our schools make it their policy to ensure that the less intellectually able get equally good academic attention as the more able? and to ensure that money is used equitably? (Have they ever asked what the 'option for the poor' might mean in terms of the intellectually poor?)

— Do schools really attack the 'success ethic' in the way they handle academic achievement? How do they publicise exam results? Do they have permanent display boards of present and old pupils' successes? How do they award prizes?

— In what ways do our schools counter the competitiveness of the exam system by positively encouraging the skills of cooperation?

— As with academic success so with every form of success; e.g. how do schools handle sport in such a way as not to create failure?

— How do schools promote and give encouragement to a whole variety of gifts not directly connected with sport or learning? And how, therefore, do schools make it known that persons are to be valued for what they are and not for what they do?

— To what extent do our schools make it their policy to accept handicapped pupils where possible?

— To what extent do our schools positively welcome pupils and teachers of a different colour and culture?

— What kind of respect do teachers require of the pupils?

— Do schools welcome and encourage parental partnership? How do they handle the false (and sometimes destructive) ambitions of parents for their children?

— How and in what way is the fundamental dynamic of the gospel, through death to resurrection (the seed dying to produce life, the least is the greatest, the first shall be last . . .) honoured in the school?

E

- How do schools express the Beatitudes in their life? How do they handle violence? Are their means of punishment in accord with the gospel? Do they in anyway demean individuals? Is punishment ever used simply to defend the dignity of authority? Are pupils ever humiliated?

- Do schools treat pupils differently because of the religious practice or non-practice of themselves or their parents?

- In what way do head teachers communicate with their staff, teachers among themselves, and staff with pupils?

- In what ways do schools help their pupils cope with the possibility of unemployment? Do they understand personal development in terms which do not depend on whether they are employed or not?

- Do our schools conceive the power of authority in the gospel terms of enabling pupils to reach their full potential or is it used simply to control?

- Do schools propose conformity as an ideal? How open are they to freedom and individuality?

- Do schools help their pupils to become critically aware of society and to acquire the critical skills needed to evaluate the systems which govern it and its underlying thinking?

- To what extent are our schools involved in the neighbourhood? Are the buildings used by the local people?

- Do our schools propose as an ideal the inter-relatedness of all peoples and all nations, or is their disposition narrowly nationalistic?

Here, perhaps, I am only beginning to touch on some of the characteristics of a gospel-endowed school, but sufficiently to indicate the kind of challenge which the community accepts when it becomes church in a school setting.

11. Aims of school

The school, therefore, aims

> at meeting pupils where they are on their faith-journeys and, in the light and power of the gospel, at accompanying them on their way towards becoming fully human.

or

> in the light of the christian faith-vision of the kingdom to help pupils grow and mature to full stature.

a. The school in its approach to each pupil endeavours to live the gospel in the way it influences everything done in the classroom and throughout school life.

b. Because I am writing about a gospel-centred school, when I put as its goal becoming fully human I see this fulfilled in Jesus Christ: he is the complete expression of what it means to be human.

c. I use the phrase very deliberately, 'meeting pupils where they are on their faith-journeys'. As I explained earlier on, I am not giving God to anybody. I am helping people, in this case pupils, discover the God who dwells within them as the source of their lives and as the one who draws them on to enjoy life in its fullness. Pupils have faith: my task is to help them to appreciate it and let it grow. I must always take care to give due respect to their faith. Because children may not be able to formulate their faith makes it no less real and I must always resist the temptation simply to impose my own set of beliefs and values on them.

d. I must also be sensitive to the total context of the pupils' lives and respect their parents' faith-stance. I must never do anything to undermine their trust in their parents. Their faith-journey began in the home, and because it may not have developed as I would have wanted makes it no less true. I have to be careful not to criticise people who do not go to Mass or pray. I have to stay within the thinking of the faith-journey.

e. Today some schools are developing a special apostolate towards parents. Very often this apostolate arises out of parental meetings organised for first holy communion. Parents have found these meetings very helpful and enriching. For the first time, perhaps, they have had the opportunity to talk over what they really believe with their own peer group. It is important, therefore, that their reflections are grounded in the reality of their everyday lives and that there is no gap between their reality and their relationship to God. A genuine faith-sharing can take place in these situations; parents find themselves affirmed and they learn to appreciate what they themselves are in fact doing for their children.

12. Conclusions

In the classroom itself the religious lesson should be religious education as I have described it earlier on. All I should like to re-emphasise here is that, though this should be the intention of the teachers, some children will receive it as evangelisation, some as catechesis, others quite simply as religious education. I should also like to remind you that evangelisation precedes catechesis.

There should always be opportunities for catechesis worked into the life of the school, especially for prayer (prayer groups) and for the celebration of the eucharist. It is absolutely essential, however, that children can withdraw from these activities freely and unobtrusively. I find it extremely difficult to think of the eucharist ever being an appropriate act of compulsory worship, either for the school as a whole or for a class. The eucharist should only be celebrated among those who are present willingly and freely; and this is not always easy to achieve, especially among younger children. On the one hand, teachers can jolly children along and easily persuade them to be present, while on the other hand, children genuinely want to please teacher. Therefore, it seems to me to be very difficult to ensure this freedom, especially in class Masses worked into the timetable. This kind of thinking, I know, leads to some very radical questions and I must refer you back to the way in which I defined catechesis.[27] For me it certainly throws a big question mark over the school assembly as an act of worship. My problem is, how can you impose worship on everybody? Worship is an act of devotion freely made by believers as a sign of their love and

[27] See above, chapter 6, section 3, 'Catechesis', p. 70.

commitment. Will individual unbelievers be helped simply by being present? Does something rub off?

Finally, it is not only worth noting but needs to be underlined again and again, that the most effective religious activity organised by schools are those occasions when the children are taken out of the school into some kind of 'retreat' experience. This is universally acknowledged. Different people will give different reasons why this experience is so valuable. For myself I would stress two things. Firstly, this experience provides a situation in which pupils can be treated individually and personally. They have an opportunity to talk about where they are on their faith-journeys, receive assurance that it is good to be where they are and be encouraged and guided to go forward. Secondly, this experience creates opportunities for the celebration of more personal liturgies and for prayer. Here I should like to make one plea with regard to liturgies. Frequently pupils experience on these occasions what are sometimes described as liturgical 'highs'. Now I see nothing wrong in such celebrations, even though they bear little relationship to their normal everyday fare. What is important, however, is that they be given an opportunity to reflect on the liturgy which they experienced as a 'high', learn how to appropriate it and make it a lasting enrichment in their lives, and, in consequence, how to cope with bad liturgical experiences. Moreover if the best is to be derived from these out-of-school experiences opportunity must be found to reflect on the experience as a whole. Those who took part in it must be helped to see what that experience is saying to their ordinary lives. The danger is that these experiences remain nice and pleasant but have no real bearing on life.

12

Parish

This is not the place, nor have I the skill or all the relevant information, for a carefully worked out presentation on the evolution and nature of a parish. However, the following paragraphs my be helpful in understanding the place of the parish in faith-sharing.

1. Natural community?

Historically the parish was a natural community: it was a given piece of territory, with a village or small town at its centre, in which the inhabitants worked and lived all their lives. The parish church was its focal point. Up to the middle of the last century, only 10% of the population lived in comparatively large towns: the other 90% fell into small natural parish units.

With the advent of the Industrial Revolution society began to change; by the year 2000 ninety percent of the world population will live in cities. Today the majority live in one place and work in another. Urbanisation has destroyed the natural community: it has led to anonymity among neighbours, and even between workers who physically rub shoulders in the same work place. In such circumstances the formation of true community presents a formidable challenge.

2. Becoming community

The christian story presents the parish ideally mirroring the universal church. 'In some ways,' says the Second Vatican Council, 'parishes represent the visible church established throughout the world' (Decree on Bishops Pastoral Office, 11). Ideally the parish should be a living community of the faithful: it should meet human-kind's profound longing not to lead inhuman lives of exile and isolation; but to find a sense of value and significance in and through belonging to God and to other human beings; and in being able to translate their need for God and for one another into worship.

At this particular point I am experiencing considerable difficulty in avoiding, on the one hand, bland idealistic notions about church and parish and in expressing, on the other hand, that rich complex reality which we call church and its particular expression we call parish. When I was a boy I was taught to define church as the perfect society. Now no matter how much I struggle to make my own the insights of the Second Vatican Council about the pilgrim nature of the church, how the church moves forward slowly step by step through the centuries exploring God's presence in the cultures of the world and deep within each human heart and, no matter how much I remember that the church is always in need of reform, some traces of the fixedness and finality of the perfect society remain. I am always imagining this complete perfect entity out there somewhere which I need to find and become part of. Yet I know this perfect society does not yet exist: there is a promise that it will one day. Meanwhile it is in the process of becoming, or rather we are in the process of becoming church, of becoming the perfect society. Matthew in chapter 18, where the nature of the church is being discussed, opens the passage with Jesus answering his disciples' question: 'Who is the greatest in the kingdom of heaven?' 'I tell you solemnly unless you change and become like little children you will never enter the kingdom of heaven' (Matthew 18:1-3). Jesus speaks of becoming children; there is a not-yet quality about church. In fact, we do not know what we shall become: the child is father of the man. In the child we may catch glimpses of what the adult will be, but if we try to programme our present hunches of what the church will be we are in danger of overlooking the transforming power of the Holy Spirit.

3. Vision and reality

It is within this thinking that we have to speak of parish. Our presentation has to combine our own experience with the visionary aspects of church which Jesus described in parables about the kingdom, hinting at a kingdom reality to which humankind is called: light, city on a hill, seed, pearl, net, yeast. Parish, moreover, has to resonate to the models of the church and be prophet, servant, herald, community, patriarchical institution. Nevertheless, parish has to meet very many people who are not yet ready for community, who do not see themselves as heralds, servants or prophets but who wish to share in the church's sacramental life. Such people (and in no way am I belittling their attitude, otherwise I would be untrue to all I have said about the faith-journey), such people see the parish as a 'service station' which provides its consumers with Mass at fixed times, confessions, instructions, baptisms, marriages, etc. I feel somewhat shamefaced in describing it in this way; I realise I am using the vocabulary of the consumer society. Nevertheless, these people form a not inconsiderable number of people who use the parish church, week by week, or maintain tenuous links with it in order to celebrate birth, marriage and death.

I would also like to add the many people who do not quite fit the above description but who frequently make up the bulk of the faithful. I am referring here to those with perhaps a very deep personal spirituality, who lead very loving lives yet are extremely individualistic. For some of them, for example, the kiss of peace is not just an embarrassment, it is a genuine stumbling-block. This group can be made up of people of all ages.

What I am emphasising here is that the parish must cater for a great variety of people: the young, the middle-aged and the elderly, single people and families, the divorced and separated, the clever and the less intellectually able, the sick, workers, and the unemployed; all sorts of people at different points on their faith-journey. The parish, therefore, is a coming together of individuals and groups, a network of communities.

In a moment I want to discuss families in a parish setting, but before I do this I would like to reflect on the parish as embodying the transforming mission of the church.

4. Transforming vision

a. Earlier on I spoke of christians being called to work at the interface or interplay between a gospel vision of life and reality alongside and with others who share that vision, and that other world which is secular and materialistic and has no place for a divine dimension.[28] As christians in this context we see ourselves as instruments of the transforming mission of the Holy Spirit, continually engaged in sharing our vision and values with others.

Now in order to be able to do this we need one another, and obviously the parish should be the place where we find mutual support and encouragement. As I reflect upon this aspect of parish, I think I would like to spell out what I understand by this mutual support and encouragement.

The work of faith-sharing at the interface between a society struggling to live by a gospel vision of life and a society which contradicts the basic presumptions of a divine dimension is very complex and full of ambiguities. In this situation christians need to return again and again to the source of their values and way of life: they need to hear the word of God and reflect upon it among themselves and celebrate eucharist together. It is in breaking the word and breaking and sharing the bread and wine that they make the gospel their own, purified of its materialistic interpretations, and are empowered to translate its values and way of living into their daily lives.

A non-gospel vision of life can be very deceptive. It can offer a very subtle alternative. The key to this materialistic vision is its reasonableness. Its proponents ground their arguments on reason. The human is the ultimate measure of everything; we are what we are by our own efforts; our value can be put in economic, social and political terms. Bland reason determines how we treat one another; reason builds our human structures, orders our network of relationships and establishes where power and privilege must lie. Such was the establishment which opposed Jesus, made up of the pharisees and sadducees. This establishment had the further advantage of claiming that God was its author; God affirmed its reasonableness! It was this reasonableness which the pharisees felt was being undermined by Jesus, and they counter-attacked: 'It is through the prince of devils, he casts out devils' (Mark 3:22). Good is characterised as evil: evil as good. The whole structure of what is good and evil is distorted and contradicted. They created their own measure of good and evil to ensure their own position, all the time appealing to God as their guarantor.

[28] See above, chapter 3, section 3, 'The community which serves', p. 47.

Similarly in our own society: we can so easily be deceived by nice people who claim to have the good of others at heart. The christian can so easily be taken in by arguments of economic, political and social reasonableness. Constantly we need to delve into our story to remind ourselves that we organise ourselves out of a human reason that has been enriched by its creator's love: that human beings have value because they belong to God and are loved with a love which outstrips human reasonableness; it was not reasonable that God should allow Jesus to be put to death by wicked men. Hence, christians working at the interface have to feel their way forward step by step, testing every inch of the way by the values of the gospel, holding up social, economic and political situations to its light. There is no authentic way forward except together in prayer and in celebrating eucharist, be we involved in sharing our faith with a would-be-convert, struggling to acquire adequate provison for the elderly, trying to support single-parent families, offering facilities for young people, etc.

b. Working out the tensions and ambiguities involved in fulfilling the mission of transforming society is part of the lives of christians. Once people have become involved in this mission there is no escape from its consequences. What is important, however, is that they should find opportunities to share the problems they encounter and support one another. Not only should they do this among fellow christians, but also with others who share their values and approach to life.

I am making this point here lest anyone should conceive of the parish as essentially a refuge from the cold winds of society, a sort of private club or a cocoon in which they can be wrapped. It is quite right that christians should seek and find peace in their faith, but the peace which is offered is that of Christ's own peace which finds expression in his cross. It is not the peace the world gives; it is the peace of being at one with the Father. This peace, although it is full of complexities, is also full of joy; but again it is the joy which belongs to Christ which has all the characteristic pain of child-bearing.

> Peace I bequeath to you,
> my own peace I give you,
> a peace the world cannot give,
> this is my gift to you.   (John 15:27)

A woman in child-birth suffers,
because her time has come;
but when she has given birth to the child she forgets the suffering
in her joy that a man has been born into the world.
So it is with you: you are sad now,
but I shall see you again, and your hearts will be full of joy,
and that joy no one will take from you.

(John 16:21-22)

5. Parents, children and sacraments

Elsewhere I have spoken about parents and the way they help their children grow in faith.[29] Here I want to deal with certain aspects of children's confession (sacrament of reconciliation) and holy communion. In order to do this I would like to make a few general remarks about sacraments as part of the life of the church.

Sacraments are rooted in life: they are celebrations of the life we lead; the 'we' here is very important. If there is no 'we' there is no church and no sacraments. In the sacraments we bring together our ordinary everyday lives with all the goodness and sinfulness they contain. We bring our words and deeds, our feelings and desires, our relationships, our loves and hates. The sacraments express our lives in a symbolic form so that we can celebrate them and worship God. When I say *symbolic form*, each sacrament has its own: for example, the bread, wine and meal of the eucharist, which is not only a sacrament but also a sacrifice; the action of being forgiven in reconciliation, or the anointing with oil in the sacrament of the sick. When I speak of *celebrating*, I mean sacraments explore our lives in the light of the life of Christ so that through and in our lives we can worship God; we can praise and thank God. Each sacrament celebrates a particular aspect of life. The sacrament of the sick, for example, explores the part that sickness plays in our lives as a means of salvation, helps us to deepen our understanding of healing, purifies us of our misconceptions, helps us to overcome our fears and strengthens us in suffering.

Sacraments, therefore, presuppose and celebrate God at work in the whole of creation, in every human being; wherever there is for-

---

[29] See above, chapter 7, section 2, 'Beginning to journey', and section 3, 'First steps', pp. 77ff; and chapter 8, section 2d, 'Personal faith story', p. 95.

giveness, love, healing, efforts at building a real community, commitment and dedication, sharing, attempts at justice, etc., there is God. The sacraments celebrate these activities, purify our understanding of them in the light of the gospel and Christ's sacrifice, and empower us to act as Christ acted. Sacraments do not bring God into the world; God is here at work already in everybody. Because children are not baptised does not mean that they do not belong to God or will not go to God if they die. Because children do not make their first confession does not mean that forgiveness is less part of their lives than of children who do.

The sacrament of reconciliation is about reconciliation in everyday life; we do wrong, offend each other, are sorry and are forgiven. This belongs to the very core of human existence, which we know to be pock-marked by the messiness of sin; but forgiveness, too, is part of life, as God's Spirit is alive in every human being encouraging each to be forgiving. The sacrament, however, takes all these elements and gives them a ritual grace-filled form which puts into words and signs the whole breadth and richness of God's reconciliation always present in daily life, purifies it of its human shoddiness in the light of Christ's forgiving sacrifice, deepens the healing love of God in the heart of believers and enables them to continue their faith-journey and be themselves instruments of reconciliation.

Take, for example, a child from a non-practising catholic home. The children are being 'prepared' in school for confession: Johnny is one of their number. The teachers feel that if they do not let Johnny make his first confession (and holy communion) they are depriving him of the richness of God's forgiveness and marking him out as one who has not made the grade. Therefore, all sorts of strategies are tried: can we get the parents 'back' (i.e. to going to Mass?); can we find an uncle or aunt who 'practises' and will act as a surrogate parent? The underlying assumption of all this well-intentioned activity is not to deprive Johnny of some immeasurable treasure; but, in fact, Johnny would not be deprived. God's love and forgiveness is as much at work in Johnny's life as it is in the lives of his catholic teachers. God is offering Johnny ways of growing in goodness and holiness different from those of his teachers, ways which at least for the time being do not include the sacraments. You see, the sacraments are immeasurably important to Johnny's teachers because they live within the christian community: their lives are fashioned around its way of believing, its way of acting and its way of worshipping in celebrating their lives sacramentally. They know that by using the sacrament of reconciliation, they are giving public testimony to God's continuing loving forgiveness throughout the human-race. In fact their practice bears witness to God at work in Johnny. This is the vocation of God's people, called to be church. What I am saying here is very important and I do not wish it to be obscured in any way. The fact that Johnny does not make his first confession and holy communion does not deprive him of God's loving activity in his life. We must always thank God for calling us to be church but we must take care never to allow ourselves by our attitudes or ways of thinking to limit the means which God uses to help people achieve their salvation. We must remember that God's saving action is limitless.

In fact, the very sincere efforts of teachers and priest to make it possible for Johnny to go to the sacraments may actually be harmful: it may damage his faith, a faith which may not have a religious expression such as is enjoyed by his teachers but is as real and as deep as theirs; this faith has, at its heart, his parents. Here, in the particular example we have used, he does experience forgiveness and is being led to forgive others.

Now it is quite possible that first sacraments could be a turning point in the lives of Johnny's parents. It may well become an occasion when they ask themselves serious questions about their lives and how they can best help Johnny grow up. It may be the moment when they remember their own religious upbringing, but this involves much more than simply their going back to 'their duties'; a real conversion has to take place and they must then receive effective support from the community. Perhaps we need to consider seriously how a parish does meet its responsibilities to such parents who, very often, feel completely lost. They have lost contact with the church, yet sufficient remains of their faith to make them worry about their children's future. Parishes may feel the need to set up some kind of guidance service to meet the very real problems which parents have, especially, at this time.

More and more in recent years we have come to conclude that preparation for first sacraments is best done in a parish setting. In this setting parents come forward freely to present their children and offer themselves to take part in their preparation. This preparation of its nature is essentially catechesis and therefore belongs to the community of believers. In recent years many dioceses have prepared their own sacramental programmes. The best known of the popular programmes are those produced by Christiane Brusselmans and Wim Saris. Central to all these programmes is the importance of involving parents; not simply so that they should teach their own children, but that they themselves should deepen their own understanding and grasp of their faith.

What do we do about the parents who do not bring their children for first sacraments? It is important that somehow or other they are made to feel that they matter and they will always be welcomed when they do come forward. This is the responsibility not just of priest and catechist but of the whole parish. Everybody is involved in reaching out to these parents; everybody is involved in praying for them.

Some teachers have felt their role in the religious formation of children under their care threatened as a result of putting the preparation for first sacraments into the parish and relying on catechists and parents. The reason, as I have explained elsewhere, is that the classroom is not generally the most suitable place for catechesis.[30] The move, in fact, does make things easier for teachers; they are relieved of the responsibility of being involved in making decisions about the readiness of children for receiving the sacraments.

The teachers do, however, have a very special part to play, at this time of preparation for the sacraments, in their religious education lessons. Classroom religious education must complement parish catechesis and not simply repeat what is going on in the parish. There is a whole world surrounding the sacraments and their reception to which children should be introduced. They need to learn, not only why there are sacraments and why people think they are important, but also about equivalent celebrations in other religions and in the lives of people who have no specific links with any religion.

6. Baptism

In various places in this book I have tried to give a picture of the church, and in this chapter to give one of the parish, and in the context

[30] See above, chapter 6, section 3, 'Ways of sharing our faith story (2)', pp. 69ff.

of parish I have also spoken of sacraments. It seems to me that only after we have some grasp of what we mean by church, the parish and sacraments can we justly begin to speak of baptism. Baptism along with confirmation and eucharist are called the sacraments of initiation; therefore, to understand them we need to know what we are initiating people into.

As Christ is sacrament so too is the church. She is God's gift to humankind. She exercises through the power of the Holy Spirit a transforming mission in the midst of humankind, she is the world's servant, she is a source of holiness for everybody, she is the home of sinners, she is prophet. All this I have already said. I have also spoken of how God is present within the life of every single human being born into the world, creating and lovingly sustaining each person, and present as one who, as it were, labours for the salvation of each with longing and compassion. Therefore it seems to me, whatever we say about baptism must take into account God's longing for the salvation of every member of the human race, 'renown, honour and peace will come to everyone who does good, Jews first, but Greeks as well. God has no favourites' (Romans 2:10-11). Hence we have to speak of very many different ways in which God brings people to God's self. God loves people no less whether they are baptised or not. This reflects very much the teaching of the second Vatican Council on the church (Lumen Gentium), which also places special emphasis on baptism.

Baptism

- celebrates God's loving and saving presence in the life of every member of the human race; 'God wants everyone to be saved' (1 Timothy 2:4)

- celebrates God's salvific activity of drawing everyone out of darkness into God's own marvellous light: '. . . he saves us by means of the cleansing waters of rebirth' (Titus 3:5)

- purifies our understanding of what being human means by declaring that people are the sons and daughters of God, endowed with a divine dignity and worthy of honour and respect

- celebrates, in consequence, that each one is able to call God by the familiar name of 'Abba' because the Holy Spirit dwells in each: '. . . the Spirit that cries "Abba, Father" ' (Galatians 4:4)

- celebrates the church receiving these persons into the companionship of its family and accepting the responsibility for their growth in faith: '. . . so all of us, in union with Christ form one body' (Romans 12:5)

- celebrates that those who are baptised are empowered by the Holy Spirit to make the mission of the church their own: 'As you (Father) sent me into the world, I have sent them into the world' (John 17:18).

It seems to me that when we begin to look at baptism in this light as the doorway into the church and reflect on what we mean by church and her mission in our world, we may well ask: 'Who would dare to offer her/himself for baptism or be responsible for offering another? And no sooner have we posed the question than we are at the heart of the christian mystery; the church is a church of sinners. Christ calls sinners to work with him for the world's transformation. It is God who knowing what we are, calls us to be church; calls us to receive God's gifts, to be the sign of God's creative and transforming love in the world: indeed to be sacrament.

Nevertheless, having said that, it does not follow that the church baptises lightly without due consideration. In the Rite of Christian Initiation of Adults the church maps out a process to be used in receiving would-be-converts into the church. This process lays special emphasis on the part the community plays; it is to welcome the newcomer into its midst, members must share with her/him what their faith means to them and listen to the would-be-convert's story of how as this time she/he is approaching the church and why — that is, to hear how God is calling this person and acting in her/his life. There are to be opportunities for a continuing evangelisation and the presentation of a systematic catechesis. The whole process is divided into stages and each stage is marked by a special rite of its own, beginning, for example, with a special liturgy to celebrate the start of the process,

The Rite of Entry. It is envisaged that the whole process may take a long time, a year or even several years. This Rite is for adult converts. However, it undoubtedly reflects clearly the mind of the church on how candidates should be prepared for baptism. We need to learn how to use it as a model for the baptism of the children by studying how to make imaginative adaptations of its many ideas which will be helpful for parents and godparents and for the community. The Rite also directs our efforts towards developing a richer post-baptismal catechesis for parents as well as children.

Baptism is, indeed, a sacrament of the church, but it also has a valid place and a function in society. Society welcomes a new member to its ranks; a new member is being inducted into the human race and that calls for celebration. And this is good; people should be given the opportunity to rejoice at the birth of children. However, we have to avoid allowing the sacrament to be used merely as a social occasion; or to allow any hint of superstition to touch its celebration as if it were a simple matter of doing something to the child.

Therefore, it is essential that the reception of this sacrament be made an occasion for a well-thought-out baptismal catechesis for parents and godparents. Today there is a great variety of ways in which this catechesis is being offered. There are parishes which gather parents who are expecting a child into little groups where catechists help them reflect on their own christian commitment in the light of the birth of a child and baptism. This approach can be very helpful for the support group which it creates. Single-parent families especially are grateful for the kind of interest which such a group offers them. Moreover parents who have, perhaps, drifted from regular practice find such a coming together tremendously strengthening in supporting the efforts they are making for the sake of their child.

Some parishes limit the number of times baptism is celebrated. This has the advantage of being able to draw people's attention to its celebration without overdoing it. It is extremely important that the people know the names of the new members of their community so that they may be aware how their responsibilities for their fellow members continually grow. These occasions, also, can be opportunities for an ongoing baptismal catechesis for the whole parish which, obviously, should include every so often the celebration of baptism during the principal Sunday eucharist.

7. Asking questions

Here I summarise in question form what I have been saying about the parish.

— What is a parish? How would you describe it?

— Who make up your parish? What kinds of people, e.g. workers, unemployed, professional people, elderly, young? What are their concerns? Which grouping predominate? Does it set the tone or give the parish a particular spirit (ethos)? How does it affect the liturgy, namely, the liturgy caters for . . .? Do you feel part of one of these groupings?

— How does the parish meet your needs? In what ways does the parish help you cope with life and meet the issues of your daily life more constructively? How does it help you face the problems arising from society today? Are you helped to reflect on the problems facing the world and society in the light of the gospel?

— How do you play your part in parish life? What particular abilities (talents) have you to offer to enrich parish life?

— How do you encourage people to play their part in the parish?

— Do you feel you have the opportunity to have your say in the life of the parish?

— To what extent do you feel yourself involved in the liturgies of the parish? Do they speak to your everyday life? Is there a wide variety of liturgies in your parishes? Who is responsible for your liturgy?

— What are the main needs of the different kinds of people who make up your parish? To what extent does the parish meet these needs, e.g. the needs of young people?

— How does the parish cope with the needs of particular groups, e.g. the elderly, the unemployed, the handicapped, foreigners (immigrants), single-parent families, the divorced, single people, etc? Does the parish ever make special provision in the liturgy for them?

— A parish is a gathering of communities. Do you feel you belong to a community in the true sense, that is, not just a group of people who come together to meet their social needs and do good works but really meet at a deep level in order to reflect upon their lives in the light of the gospel and follow out those reflections in practice?

— Do you feel your parish is characterised by prayer?

— In what ways is the whole parish encouraged to be involved in the sacraments of baptism, marriage and of the sick, e.g. is the parish, at least, told the names of its new members, the progress of its sick?

— What provision is made to help the elderly housebound and families who have chronically sick or disabled members? Who looks after this sphere of parish life? Is this care extended, as far as possible, to the whole district and not just to parishioners?

— What process does the parish adopt to monitor the care offered by the relevant agencies to those in need, the sick, the unemployed, those on the poverty line, etc? Are those who need special help being properly catered for? Does the parish offer support to doctors, nurses, teachers, social workers, etc. to help them work effectively? Who has the responsibility for this area in the parish?

— How are issues of peace and justice handled by the parish? How does it keep them firmly before people's minds? Who is responsible for this area?

— Is the parish sensitive to the different places where its members may be on their faith-journey?

— What kind of help does the parish offer to parents who may have given up coming to church but are struggling to make efforts at the time of their children's first Holy Communion?

— Does the parish welcome strangers and new families? How is this welcome expressed?

— Why have parishes? What are they meant to do? What in fact do they do?

13

Prayer

Perhaps in no other area can I sum up some strands of my faith-journey, and conclude this book than by saying a few words on prayer.

During all the years of my growing-up I prayed, but prayer was extremely hard. I was haunted by the catechism answer, which I learnt at school, about distractions. How often I repeated the Our Father and Hail Mary to make certain they were said without my mind wandering on to other things. Prayer, I accepted, was raising up my mind and heart to God; therefore it could not be anything but sinful to let my mind stray from the words I was saying. I hear you saying 'scruples'; scruples there were in abundance. I was worshipping a very exacting God.

It is extremely difficult to be precise as to when changes began to take place in my faith-journey without writing at much greater length than I intend to do here. It was well into the second part of my life before I came to realise that God's gentleness and compassion had given me a new insight into God's exacting nature. Prayer is undoubtedly raising up my mind and heart to God, but this is only one aspect of prayer.

Central to my understanding of my relationship to God is the truth which gradually emerged within me, and continues to emerge with all its implications, that everything that is good, every strand of love, compassion, peace, joy, truth, faith, patience, gentleness, hope, mercy I find in myself is God's gift. All is gift. Prayer is gift, God's gift.

The problem I had always been struggling with was that I believed that everything depended on my own efforts. I was a non-achiever. There could be no progress. I was a failure. And then I discovered everything was gift; even my efforts to pray were gift. That phrase,

'Because you loved me, you have made me lovable', became the source of my reflections. I was nothing; I had nothing which I had not received. Slowly, therefore, I began to see the need to feel my way towards an inner poverty; and so I became involved in a new facet of the faith-journey, the journey into poverty. I began to realise that the heart of prayer lay in poverty but what that poverty is I do not yet know. It would make this section too long to explore with you the odd corners I find in myself on this journey.

Poverty, inner need, is at the heart of prayer. I need to be loved in order to be able to love. Two people in love make possible, bring into being, evoke each other's love. Their loving is praying.

A friend of mine helped me into an understanding of the resurrection appearances in the context of prayer. In these appearances Jesus, the risen Lord, was educating his friends in a new kind of presence. They had lived with him, travelled with him, slept alongside him, knew what he liked to eat, watched him die. Now he came to them in a completely new way. He was making himself part of their inner lives. Paul puts the resulting relationship like this: 'I live now not with my own life but with the life of Christ who lives in me' (Galatians 2:20). In the resurrection appearances, Jesus is feeling his way into their lives. How he longs to be with them! He finds them where they are: eating a meal together, two of them running away from the disaster of his death, Mary Magdalene looking for a dead body, Thomas despondent in his doubts. He comes to each, making no demands, just seeking entry into their lives. Jesus comes to each, shows himself the same Jesus as of old, yet different. Mary Magdalene thought him a gardener, the apostles a ghost, the disciples on the road to Emmaus did not recognise the stranger, and in that exquisitely beautiful scene in John's last chapter, the comment is made: 'None of the disciples were bold enough to ask, "Who are you?" they knew quite well it was the Lord' (John 21:12). He was the same Jesus yet different. As the risen Lord he was able to be one with these people he loved in a way which they could never have imagined: 'things beyond the mind of men; all that God has prepared for those who love him' (1 Corinthians 2:9). Jesus became one with them. They prayed him into their lives.

Prayer is responding to Jesus feeling his way into my life. Prayer is simply the relationship between myself and God through Jesus Christ, a living relationship because it is brought about and kept in being by the Holy Spirit. To live within this relationship is prayer. As God's presence in my life is God's gift, so is prayer God's gift.

If you want to pray, ask God to give you that gift. If you want to know how to introduce children to prayer, ask God! Ultimately, and I mean ultimately, all is gift!

This book has had children for its focal point, though I trust it has become apparent that we, adults, can only help children if we attend to our own faith-journey. If our community is to grow richer in faith the main thrust of its apostolic endeavours must be put into adult education and formation, because the responsibility of helping children grow in faith belongs to all of us. The more we, adults, are in touch with the God who dwells within the very depth of our beings and allow ourselves to yield to the way God draws us to God's self the more we will find the resources within ourselves to become attentive to God's presence and activity in our world and in all those who people it and, in particular, in the children we are trying to be with as they grow in faith. Prayer evokes our sensitivity to the divine presence within the familiar aspects of our life and also where it is hidden within what seems alien to our own ideas of what it means to be religious. It is in and through prayer that we are able to answer the question, 'Where is your God?'

One day when the preacher returned from prayer, a member of his company asked him, 'Where is God? Tell us where is God's secret dwelling place?' 'Listen carefully, my friends, I'll tell you where God hides.' He closed his eyes and quietly described that secret place. His companions made him repeat what he said till it was fixed in their minds; then grasping their staves they set out, praying as they went. Days passed. Slowly they returned one by one. And as they came in a smile of recognition filled the face of each. The preacher had described the place where they all lived.

Bibliography

This book is the fruit of my personal experience. Part of this experience has grown out of listening to lectures and sermons, taking part in discussions, listening to other people's faith stories, and taking part in innumerable conversations; another part from reading books, magazines, etc. Now I am faced, here, with what I find the rather daunting task of providing a bibliography.

The professional religious educator is not at the top of my list of those for whom I have written this book, though she/he is on it. If such a person is looking for a bibliography I can only recommend him/her to consult a book like Thomas H. Groome, *Christian Religious Education*, Harper and Row, 1980. I have personally found this most helpful among recent books as summing up many facets of my own thinking.

For books which have specific reference to the religious education scene in this country I refer you to the bibliography in R.M. Rummery, *Catechesis and Religious Education in a Pluralist Society*, E.J. Dwyer, Sydney, 1975.

When I reflect back to the beginnings of my introduction to this whole field of faith-sharing names like Fathers Jungmann, Hoffinger and Van Caster come back to my mind; I am well aware of my debt to them. I remember too the vast amount of written material produced about schools and can recount much of the development of the concept of religious education as we use it in schools today. Little of all this have I reflected in this Bibliography. I have taken a number of headings and suggested the names of some books under each, books which have helped me.

IMAGE OF GOD

Abbot, W. (ed,), *Documents of Vatican II*, Geoffrey Chapman, 1966: especially on the Church and Revelation

Baum, G., *Man Becoming*, Herder and Herder, 1971

Danielou, J., S.J., *The Lord of History*, Longman, 1958

Fransen, Piet, *Divine Grace and Man*, Mentor Omega, 1964

Gutierrez, G., *A Theology of Liberation*, SCM Press, 1971

Moran, Gabriel, *Theology of Revelation*, Burns and Oates, 1967

Rahner, K., *Sacramentum Mundi, Theological Investigations*, Darton Longman & Todd, 1966-82

HUMAN

Baum, G., *Man Becoming*, Herder and Herder, 1971

Berger, Peter et al, *The Homeless Mind*, Penguin, 1974

Bruggemann, W., *The Prophetic Imagination*, Fortress Press, 1978

Bruggemann, W., *The Creative Word*, Fortress Press, 1982

Cox, Harvey, *The Secular City*, Collier Macmillan, 1965

Crossan, John D., *The Dark Interval: Towards a Theology of Story*, Argus Communications, 1975

Fromm, E., *To Have or to Be*, Jonathan Cape, 1978

Schillebeeckxx, E., *God Among Us*, SCM, 1982

Schoonenberg, Piet, *Man and Sin*, Sheed and Ward, 1965

Wiesel, Elie, *The Town Beyond the Wall*, Robson Books, 1982

CHURCH: PARISH

Brusslemans, C., *We Celebrate the Eucharist*, Silver Burdett

Clark, David, *Basic Communities — Towards an Alternative Society*, SPCK, 1977

Congar, Yves, *Lay People in the Church*, Geoffrey Chapman, 1959

Dulles, Avery, *Models of the Church*, Gill Macmillan, 1976

Bishops of England and Wales, *The Easter People*, St Pauls, 1980

Lash, N. (ed.), *Authority in the Changing Church*, Sheed and Ward, 1968

Congregation of Divine Worship, *Rite of Christian Initiation of Adults*, 1972

Saris, W., *Towards a Living Church*, Collins, 1980

Schillebeeckxx, E., *Christ the Sacrament*, Sheed and Ward, 1963

EVANGELISATION : CATECHESIS : RELIGIOUS EDUCATION

Sacred Congregation for the Clergy, *General Catechetical Directory*, 1971

Paul VI, *Evangelisation (Evangelii Nuntiandi)*, 1974

John Paul II, *Catechesis in Our Time (Catechesi Tradendae)*, 1979

Nichols, Kevin, *Cornerstone*, St Pauls, 1978

Italian and Australian Episcopal Conferences, *The Renewal of the Education of the Faith*, 1970

Donovan, Vincent, *Christianity Rediscovered*, SCM, 1978

Moran, Gabriel, *God Still Speaks*, Burns and Oates, 1967

O'Leary, D.J. and Sallnow, T., *Love and Meaning in Religious Education*, OUP, 1982

FAITH : MEANING : DEVELOPMENT

Fowler, J.W., *Stages of Faith*, Harper and Row, 1981

Gallagher, Michael P., *Help my Unbelief*, Veritas, 1983

Lane, D., *The Experience of God*, Veritas, 1981

Moran, G., *Religious Education Development*, Winston Press, 1983

Phenix, P.H., *Realms of Meaning*, McGraw-Hill, 1974

Westerhoff, J.H., *Will our Children have Faith?*, Seabury Press, 1976

Index